W9-AWR-347

BUILD A BETTER YOU
—STARTING NOW!
Volume 1

BUILD A BETTER YOU —STARTING NOW!

Volume 1

DR. WILLIAM J. COOK, JR.

WILLIAM G. FITZ-HUGH

LOLA GREEN

MARK VICTOR HANSEN

ROBERT H. HENRY

JOAN JEWETT

CHARLES E. "TREMENDOUS" JONES

WILLIAM J. McGRANE, C.P.A.E.

NAOMI R. RHODE, R.D.H.

RAY SONNENBERG

SUZY SUTTON

DR. BILL E. THOMAS

PETER H. THOMAS

DR. JAMES J. TUNNEY

DONALD M. DIBLE, EDITOR

SHOWCASE PUBLISHING COMPANY
Fairfield, California

Library of Congress Catalog No. 79-63064
ISBN 0-88205-200-4

Copyright © 1979 by Donald M. Dible
All rights reserved. No part of this book may be repro-
duced or transmitted in any form or by any means, electronic or mechanical, including photocopying, recording,
or by any information storage and retrieval system, without permission in writing from the Publisher.

Printed in the United States of America

Showcase Publishing Company
3422 Astoria Circle
Fairfield, California 94533

Distributed to the retail trade by
Hawthorn Books, Inc.

First Printing

TABLE OF CONTENTS

PREFACE

The publication of this inaugural volume of *Build a Better You—Starting Now!* is a very special event, for it marks the launching of not only a new series of books, but the launching of a new publishing company as well. I'd like to take a moment to tell you just a little bit about this volume, this series, and about our publishing company.

First, a word about this volume. Here you have the opportunity to benefit from the motivating, inspiring, and enthusiasm-generating ideas of fourteen of North America's most exciting platform personalities—speakers whose messages are heard in person or on cassette by hundreds of thousands of people every year. Now, you have the opportunity to read transcripts of their most popular talks or share their most carefully thought-out ideas and discoveries as they commit their observations to the printed page. These messages are now available for the first time in book form. *Build a Better You—Starting Now! Volume 1* is that book—the first in a planned series of 26 volumes.

Next, a word about this series. A full year of motivational, inspirational and self-help "vitamins." That's the idea behind this 14-chapters-per-volume, 26-volume series: A full year's supply of mental nourishment to be read (consumed) at the rate of one chapter per day for 365 days. (Volume 26 will contain 15 chapters making a total of 365 chapters.)

Drawing from among the best of the tens of thousands of established and fast-rising stars in the self-help speaking field, this series is dedicated to bringing to wider and wider audiences throughout the world the vital message: You can Build a Better You—Starting Now! (given proper guidance) if you are truly dedicated to making it happen.

Finally, a word about the Showcase Publishing Company. Showcase was launched by the founders of The Entrepreneur Press, an eight-year-old company dedicated to publishing books for new and small business owners. (One of our titles, *Up Your OWN Organization!—A Handbook on How to Start and Finance a New Business* has sold more than 100,000 copies.) *All* of the customers of The Entrepreneur Press are interested in self-help information. However, as we came to appreciate that a far larger audience existed for self-help information directed at personal development, the decision was made to start a new company dedicated to serving this larger audience.

As a public speaker myself (I regularly present more than 100 seminars a year), and as a member of several associations of public speakers, I realized that my fellow speakers could provide an enormous amount of material for the new audience we had chosen to serve. It was at this point that we decided to start Showcase. We sincerely hope you will agree that we did the right thing.

Should you, or someone you know, be interested in contributing material to one of our future volumes, please don't hesitate to write to us. We look forward to hearing from you.

DONALD M. DIBLE
Publisher and Editor-in-Chief
SHOWCASE PUBLISHING COMPANY
3422 Astoria Circle
Fairfield, California 94533

BUILD A BETTER YOU —STARTING NOW!
Volume 1

Dr. WILLIAM J. COOK, Jr.

Dr. William J. Cook, Jr.—professional motivator, business executive, educator, and author. He is president of Colonial Management Association, Inc., a Lowder Associates Company affiliate, headquartered in Montgomery, Alabama, and of Colonial Regency in Nashville, Tennessee. A native of Alabama, he earned his A.B. from Jacksonville State University and his M.A. and Ph.D. from Auburn University, specializing in communications, literature, and human values. From 1969 until 1975, he was an assistant vice president and associate professor at Auburn University at Montgomery. He resigned this position to pursue a full time career in business as a senior executive. From 1975 to 1977, he served as a vice president and assistant to the president of Hudson-Thompson, Inc., a large food distribution company.

Dr. Cook is a member of the editorial boards of two journals and is the author of two books and several articles associated with language, literature, human values, and motivation. He is a member of the board of directors at the Alabama Retail Association; a member of the American Management Association, the Modern Language Association, Rotary International, and several other professional and civic organizations.

A Distinguished Military Graduate, he served as a Regular Army officer 1960-1963, with the Second Infantry Division.

He has been named to Phi Kappa Phi; Outstanding Young Men of America; Who's Who in Alabama; the Dictionary of International Biography; Outstanding Young Educators of America; Who's Who in the South and Southwest; Contemporary Authors; and Who's Who in Finance and Industry, as well as others. He serves on the Advisory Council for the Humanities at Auburn University, and the Advisory Council for the School of Business, University of Montevallo; Alabama's Business Advisory Forum, and as president of Alabama's Advisory Council for Career Education.

You may contact Dr. Cook by writing to Colonial Management Association, Inc., Post Office Box 2571, Montgomery, Alabama 36105 or telephoning (205) 265-7073.

THE TRUE NATURE OF MOTIVATION

by Dr. WILLIAM J. COOK, Jr.

A Matter of Motivation

The subject is motivation. A very familiar subject to anyone reading this book. Millions of dollars and millions of
hours are spent each year by businesses and by aggressive
individuals in an effort either to discover the secrets of
motivation or to translate these secrets into personal
achievement or success. Those who seek to understand
the "mysteries" of motivation or to achieve for themselves some degree of motivation are to be con-
gratulated—first, because the seeking itself indicates
a positive, self-responsible view of life; and, second, because motivation is indeed the beginning point of any
achievement. So great is the demand for motivational
materials and programs that recently a veritable motiva-

tional industry has sprung up. Offerings include a variety of books, cassettes, films, and seminars that feature a variety of approaches to motivation, ranging from the sublime to the ridiculous. It is not my purpose here to pass judgment on any of these programs or approaches; however, I would point out that, in most instances, these attempts at motivation provide at best only temporary motivation. The "high" is usually followed by a sustained "low" until another infusion of motivation can be found somewhere. Some say that this is the nature of motivation—"roller-coaster"—but I believe true motivation is more permanent, longer lasting—in fact, unstoppable.

The basic problem is that most people—including some "motivators"—don't really understand the nature of motivation. I'll be the first to admit that, even after years of study and practical observation, there are many things about the workings of motivation that I don't understand either. The human personality is a very complex thing. But I do know something about the *nature* of motivation, and that, before anything else, must be the basis for all our understanding. It is the real nature of motivation which I will discuss here.

There are two fundamental facts about motivation which must be accepted at the outset of our discussion. The first is that motivation cannot be reduced to a formula, nor can it be programmed, nor is it something which can be applied or taken in doses, nor is it always consistent in its particulars. It is, rather, simple and complex, art and science, emotional and rational because it involves a myriad of human personalities. But to the degree that human personalities have common characteristics—human nature, as we call it—the general nature of motivation is always the same.

The second fact which must be understood about motivation is that it is relatively constant; that is, it is always present in every person. A quick look at the root of the word reveals that motivation has to do with "moving" by providing a "motive," and we are moved even to inactivity or apathy. The commonly held view of motivation, however, is that it is something which can be turned on and off at will, and it is associated with "moving and grinning," enthusiasm, and success. So we see a "super" salesperson, a real achiever, the number one producer, and we say, "That person is really motivated." Then we see a last-place salesperson who is lethargic, listless, and late, and we wonder, "Why isn't he motivated?" The fact is that both are motivated—but in opposite directions. I have come to believe that all of us are motivated all the time—even while we sleep—subconsciously. The only difference between the "winner" and the "loser" is the attitude of motivation (that is, positive or negative) and the degree of motivation (high or low).

So the problem is not just motivating ourselves or others; it is, rather, providing positive motivation in realistic proportions and in human terms. We can do this only if we understand the fundamental nature of motivation, which is tantamount to understanding the fundamental nature of people.

A Matter of Perspective

The first characteristic of motivation is: motivation is a matter of *perspective*. And the immediate complicating factor is the old saying that "no two people see the same thing the same way." That adage is more easily said than accepted because every one of us is limited in our perception of reality, yet we tend to hold to our view as if it were the only one or, more likely, the only right one. But there is more involved here than a simple argument over specific cases—it is a total world perspective which influences everything we do or do not do.

Psychologists tell us that we can perceive objects and qualities in three categories: things, people, ideas. The possible divergence of perceptions increases dramatically from things to people and even more from people to ideas. In that category, it is probably true that no two people have ever been able to share exactly the same idea; we deal in approximations. To this list I would add a fourth category, a category even less absolute than that of ideas. You see, we also perceive feelings—and that is the most important category of all. In fact, selling, managing, motivating, and communicating are all basically emotional activities. It is for that reason that the best salespersons, managers, motivators, and communicators are those people who are able to perceive feelings accurately and to respond sympathetically.

People see differently for three reasons. First, there is the obvious matter of *capacity*. Mentally, physically, perhaps even spiritually, each of us has a different quality and kind of capacity. Quite often capacity is responsible not only for how well we do a job, but it is often the determining factor in whether or not we even make the attempt. For example, at present I am physically incapable of pole-vaulting seventeen feet; perhaps that explains why I am not moved to enter Olympic competition. And if that obligation were forced on me by some perverse diety or the like, I would probably suffer from extreme anxiety and depression.

I remember vividly my first real lesson in how people see differently. As an operations officer for my infantry division, I was responsible for the tactical maneuvers of about thirty sizable units. My assistant, who was also my driver, was a highly intelligent, dedicated youngster; he had been with me for almost two years. Our tactical map during an exercise was filled with hundreds of colored map tacks, each color representing a different kind of unit. After one such exercise was over, I asked him to sort the tacks by color and replace them in the appropriate bins. Some time later, I noticed that, for all his painstaking effort, the tacks were thoroughly mixed—all colors in every bin. The problem? You guessed it. He was color blind. Red to him would always be grey; so would blue and green and just about every other color. I learned that day that it is possible to know someone very well and still be oblivious to obvious incapacities. I still do not know what happened to the troops in the field.

Second, there is the matter of *experience*. And I do not speak of merely having done something, but of the retained wisdom and perspective arising out of that experience. Our cumulative experience usually creates at any specific time an inescapable point of view. Whether I have twenty years' experience on a job or one year's experience twenty times does not alter the fact that I see everything from that perspective. Furthermore, my experience may be biased, prejudiced, totally inaccurate, contrary to all reason—but, if it is my experience, it assuredly gives me my perspective. Obviously, then, in a variegated society such as ours, major problems in motivation arise from the diverse backgrounds of experience and consequent misunderstandings and conflicts, unless sensitivity to and appreciation of a variety of experiences is mutually shared.

My favorite example of how widely differing perspectives can result in unbelievably diverse interpretations concerns time distortion. We all know that time contracts with pleasure and expands with pain. But what of the conflicting perspectives of, say, parent and young child? Picture this: you are thirty-five; your daughter is five. You are driving to see grandmother, who lives three hours away. After two hours on the road, there is a gentle tap on the shoulder and your little girl asks, "How much farther?" Realizing miles mean nothing to her (because of experience), you say sagely, "It's only an hour." The next statement from the youngster is always the same: "But I can't wait." But, being the wise parent you are, you know anybody can wait one hour for anything; so you tell her to be quiet and wait: "It's only an hour." Wrong! In terms of life experience, you have lived seven times longer than the child—your little hour is *seven* hours to her. Her perspective makes it so. And so it is indeed with all of us. Tell me what you will; I will believe and act based on my experience.

The third factor contributing to perspective is *needs*. If this factor is not the most personal, it is the most private. But it is also probably the strongest factor in determining perspective. Need can obscure traditional values, justify erratic behavior, provoke inordinate ambition—in short, it can, for as long as it persists, dominate perspective.

We know that there are needs characteristic of all people—basic human needs; these definitely have a bearing on perspective. They will be discussed in the section on values. But the needs we are concerned with here are those more temporary needs that arise in the course of everyday living in our pressurized and complex world of economics, social obligations, competition, expectations, and dreams. As with capacity and experience, all of us have widely differing needs. And we are all motivated at different times by different needs.

For example, as a vice president of a university, I was responsible for research, contracts, and grants. On one occasion, I was called by a federal agency with a renewal acceptance on a three-million-dollar contract. Excitedly, I called the director of the project (incidentally, his salary was in the $25,000 range) and told him the good news. His reply was dumbfounding. He only wanted to know about his travel check for $62.00. I was talking about millions; he was interested in merely a few dollars. Why? It was the twenty-ninth day of the month; he could not ride the float for two more days at his bank; he needed money to buy food for his family that day. That morning he saw through the eyes of a provider for seven dependents, not as a project director. His perspective was based solely on his need; and, although it was temporary, that need overrode all other considerations until it was filled.

These three factors—*capacity, experience,* and *needs*—are the reasons for the innumerable perspectives from which people see. Understanding why or how these perspectives exist is not as important as recognizing that they are instrumental in motivation—for us as well as for others.

A Matter of Values

The second characteristic of motivation is: motivation is a matter of *values.* This particular tenet became obvious in the discussion of the role of needs in forming perspective. But, in a larger sense, values are a result of the permanent and universal human needs—as well as a lifetime of teaching, beliefs, and trial-and-error living.

By now the name Abraham Maslow is almost a household word. It was he who first graphically depicted the universal needs and the ensuing values.

Proceeding from the base, he explained first our fundamental biological needs—food, water, shelter; then the need for safety and security—now most often physical safety and economic security; then our social need—gregarious creatures need to be with others; then the need for respect—including, most of all, self-respect; and

9

finally the need for self-actualization—the need to be what we really are. His famous pyramid looked something like this:

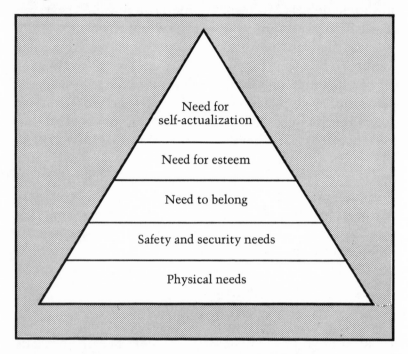

Need for
self-actualization

Need for esteem

Need to belong

Safety and security needs

Physical needs

Practically speaking, for each of us there is one predominant level in which we operate most of the time; but as need circumstances change, we are susceptible to corresponding changes in values. For example, a middle-income executive may characteristically move at the esteem level, but if his job is threatened, he quickly moves to the level of safety and security, and his sense of values follows. If his house is destroyed, his physical needs easily become the moving factor in his life. Several years ago, a well-known prime minister was kidnapped and held essentially without food for several weeks. Upon being freed, his first request was for a piece of plain bread. At that moment, he admitted, "Until now, I've never known how good bread is." Needs change and so do values.

One of the basic problems in moving people is recognizing their level of need, hence, something of their values. The best salespeople and managers—for that matter, the best fathers and mothers, the best husbands and wives—are those who can discern need levels. Unfortunately, most of us give little thought to the needs of others—we're too busy with our own.

Another children's story: a friend of mine took his six-year-old son to Disney World and in three days spent almost two hundred dollars on him. As they were leaving, the boy asked for a seventy-five-cent balloon. The father refused, pointing out emphatically that he had spent a small fortune on the kid. The six-year-old cried all the way to Lake City. Now he wants to be a balloon salesman—and he will be. Why? Because not only was the seventy-five cents not spent on him, neither was the two hundred dollars. It was all done by a father who needed esteem so badly that he could not see the security needs of his son. While he is bragging to his buddies at work, his boy is dreaming of capturing the world's balloon market.

People are moved according to their values. Their values are determined by their needs. Some insurance companies used to teach their agents that there were seven motivating needs: profit, pride, pleasure, caution, utility, love, and ambition. And I suppose that in one way or another each of these needs can be placed somewhere on Maslow's scale. But however we categorize needs, it must be remembered that they are the basis of values, and values are a key factor in motivation.

A Matter of the Human Dimension

The third characteristic of motivation is: motivation is a matter of the *human dimension*. Unfortunately, we live at a time in which people are thought of in mostly physical, external dimensions, so attempts at motivation are also most often external. Success, whatever that is, is described in glowing, material terms. Motivational appeals are made on the basis of swimming pools, luxury cars, recreational vehicles, round-the-world trips, pockets full of money, expensive clothes, and sleeping till ten o'clock in the morning. And, of course, to be successful, you must look successful—so we exercise; diet; get tanned, manicured, and coiffured; and learn good manners and polite conversation. But I have known people who had all these things—who, from all appearances, were the epitome of success—and who were miserable inside.

The ancient Greeks had the idea that we were comprised of three parts, inseparable in this life but distinct nevertheless: the *soma,* or the body; the *psyche,* or the intellect; and the *pneuma,* or the spirit. I believe this view is also consistent with Christian theology. The body is important, obviously, and must be sustained and nurtured in good health, but it is not the most important. The intellect is important and, furthermore, is tremendously powerful because it has an amazing control over the body, and not just in voluntary motor activity. For example, in England a few years ago, the physicians went out on strike and the mortality rate dropped eighty percent—people thought they were well and quit dying.

Even so, the third component of the human being— the spirit—is the source of motivation, for it provides both the will to do and the power to do.

It is because of that will and power that I am not simply a creature which reacts to external stimuli. And I am not slavishly subject to the conditioning of external forces. In fact, I have the power even to control the circumstances. Therefore, there is for me no such thing as luck, fate, chance, or magic. I make my own destiny and I control my life—even when I refuse to control it. I can will to be an *effect*—to allow things to happen to me; or I can will to be a *cause*—to make things happen.

The single most important truth in motivation—whether it be the motivation of ourselves or others—is simply that each of us is a *cause*—or can be. External motivation, whether reward or punishment, is at best temporary, at worst fraudulent, always disillusioning.

A Matter of Self-Determination

The fourth characteristic of motivation is: motivation is a matter of *self-determination*. Because true motivation is internal, it must also originate internally within the heart and will. I have grown somewhat weary of bonuses and incentive awards as motivating gimmicks—they should be used to reward positive motivation, not to create it, because none of these things, rewards or punishments, is guaranteed to produce results. Only one thing will do that. Without fail. In every instance. Since the world began, never has this one thing failed in its power to motivate. What is this remarkable device? Purpose.

Real purpose renders incidental external rewards or incentives. I have come to realize that I cannot motivate anyone, nor can they me; but we each motivate ourselves through our own discovery of purpose. I can assist you in finding your purpose by offering three suggestions.

The first is this: You must learn to love yourself. Now that may seem a bit strange, asking you to love yourself, but the majority of people somehow have been convinced that they are not worth liking—usually because they correlate performance with self-worth. Recently, as a part of a State Department of Education study, I helped develop self-concept profiles on a group of high-school seniors. An optimum score—one indicating a healthy attitude toward self-worth—was 100. I saw one score as low as 3; another, 11; another, 13. The average score was 47.5. These teenagers had a distressingly low self-concept only because they had been taught to degrade, dislike, and even punish themselves for inadequacies, mistakes, and failure. Like most of us, the first thing they heard as a child was a threatening "no," somehow connected with the idea that the violation of a rule, or failure in any attempt, or simply not measuring up constituted grounds for self-hatred. They had been taught that what we do or do not do is inherently connected to what we are worth. So they grew up, like so many others, with a failure complex—afraid to risk success for fear of losing their self-worth, because every time they fail they are, in their own estimation, worth a little less.

The late Robert Kennedy said that, in order to succeed greatly, one must be able to fail greatly. There is an old, perhaps apocryphal, story about Thomas Edison. It tells of Edison when he had already failed over nine hundred times in his attempts to make an electric light. His friends asked him if he was not discouraged. His reply was, "No. No. Now I know nine hundred things that will not work."

Most people who try are in the rejection business; every day they set themselves up to fail. And I believe if they do not fail at least forty percent of the time, they are not trying hard enough. Without failure, there is no reach, no achievement, no excellence, no joy. A person who does not have a healthy self-love cannot succeed because he cannot fail. But a successful person knows that even if he should fail totally—one hundred percent of the time—he is still worth more than the wealth of the entire world. And this awareness is the first step in the discovery of both a personal purpose and a professional calling.

The second prerequisite of discovering your purpose is to clean up your vocabulary. I don't mean eliminating profanity or the like, but removing certain words such as: "should," "must," "have to," and other such words which imply necessary and restricting obligation to everything and everyone but yourself. As a person, before you decide who and what that person is, implant this truth deeply within your heart and mind: There is *nothing* you have to do; *nothing* you should do; *nothing* you ought to do. Now I know your first reaction to that advice may be to call it and me irresponsible. But that is the most responsible and the truest advice you have ever had.

Let me tell you why. You can waste your entire life doing what you think you have to do—and be miserable doing it. I knew a senior official at a major university. We had coffee together each Monday morning. Every time he would greet me with, "This job is killing me. I hate it. One of these days I'm going back to the farm." He did go back to the farm—when he was sixty-five and retired. And three months later, in a cornfield, he died of a heart attack. He had lived three months. Recently, at a cocktail party, I talked with a thirty-seven-year-old man who was in the real estate business. He hated the profession and was only interested in making a lot of money before his fiftieth birthday so he could then retire and do what he wanted to do. He was an extremely foolish man. I told him to do what he wanted to do now—to redeem those thirteen years in living, not waste them in a miserable slavish existence.

15

And that same advice I offer seriously and urgently to you. Do what you want to do, now! Do what you are, now! If your present vocation or company or business situation is not you, get out of it as soon as you can—and make everybody happy, including yourself. If your present job is not you, do everybody a favor and quit; then do yourself a bigger favor and be what you are. Do you know why most people are afraid to do that? Simply this: if they fail doing what someone else has imposed on them or what they think they "have to" do, then they have somebody to blame. If they are doing what they want to do, they have no one to blame for failure but themselves. But, then, come to think of it, they have no one else to credit for their success, which is bound to come if they do what they are.

I taught thousands of students at the university who should not have been there, hundreds more who were majoring in subjects they hated. Why? Parental pressure. I remember one student in particular whose dad was a pharmacist and who was thus compelled to be a pharmacist also—to continue the family tradition and business. But junior was a fisherman at heart; he loved fishing more than anything in the world; and he knew more about it than just about anybody in the world. But he got his degree in pharmacy, went to a nearby town, and opened the family's second drugstore. He was not only miserable, he was a mediocre pharmacist because it was not him—he didn't love it. When he reached thirty-five, he came to his senses and realized he didn't have to do something he despised. So he sold his store, moved to the Gulf Coast, and bought two fishing boats. You guessed it. He is now the best commercial fisherman in the whole area—and he is the second happiest person I know. And he can be the second happiest person you know if you have the courage to do what you are.

Third, as a preliminary step in discovering purpose, we must increase our vocabulary, and our thinking, by two words. I like to think that these words can somehow be emblazoned on our foreheads, so each morning, as we look in the mirror, we have them reinforced in our hearts. The words are "no limits." And I believe that there are no limits on you but you. Sometimes in executive seminars, I ask the participants to begin writing down things they want to do during their life—no restrictions of any kind. Invariably, they all begin very enthusiastically, gleefully in fact, to record all the things they have dreamed of doing; but, then, something happens. It never fails. They begin crossing out some of the entries. When I ask why, the reply is always, "I can't really do that." My response is, "That's right. You can't. But only because you marked through it." If you think you can't, you can't. Think like a loser, and you'll be a loser. Think like a winner; be a winner.

I have taken a great deal of time to discuss this characteristic of motivation because I believe this is the point at which most people acquiesce to negative motivation—because they are afraid to fail, or because they think they have to do something, or because they impose restrictive limits on themselves. And I have intentionally made the discussion here very personal with the thought that you might not only gain an understanding of motivation but maybe even be positively motivated yourself. Because with you and me, as with everyone else, motivation can never be anything but self-originating.

A Matter of the Now

Finally, the last characteristic of motivation I will discuss in this chapter is: motivation is a matter of the *now*.

Now I know that we have sought to motivate through goal-setting devices. And these techniques are in some situations employed very successfully. In fact, I believe that everyone should have a personal five-year plan projecting every area of his life. But goals, quotas, and objectives are not motivational tools. Motivation is now—and only now.

How unfortunate that most people live in one of two other places. Some live in the past. They live there for two reasons: either because they relish the "good ol' days" or because they cannot escape a past failure or mistake. The first group substitutes the past for the present so they give up the goodness of the now; the second group is so consumed by regret that there is no goodness in the now.

Some other people live in the future. Mostly they are terrorized by all the catastrophic things that could happen to them. They live in anxiety, under constant stress, and die early from heart attack. Ironically, ninety-five percent of the things they worried about never happen. So they are killed by invisible monsters.

Neither those who live in the past nor those who live in the future really live because living can happen only in the now. The renaissance theme of *"carpe diem"* was wiser than we thought. "Seize the day," they said; distill from every minute of life all the good in it. Learn from the past, prepare for the future, but live now. Positive motivation cannot occur when the appeal is to past glory or failure or to future reward or punishment, and for one simple reason: the only time anyone is motivated is *now*, just at the moment he is living.

These, then, are the five characteristics of motivation: motivation is a matter of perspective; motivation is a matter of values; motivation is a matter of human dimension; motivation is a matter of self-determination; motivation is a matter of the now.

ROBERT H. HENRY

Robert Henry, from Auburn, Alabama, is one of the fast-est rising stars on the American platform. A Southerner by birth, nature, inclination, upbringing, and inspiration, Henry is at a complete loss to explain why he lived in Washington, D.C. for five years.

Henry attended public schools in his native state of Mississippi. He graduated from the University of South-ern Mississippi in 1958 with a Bachelor of Science degree in Speech and Marketing. While at Southern, Henry was active in campus affairs, serving as president of his class for three years and president of eight different campus organizations.

After graduation, he was involved in direct sales for several years and won two outstanding salesman awards.

Henry returned to school to pursue a career in pharmacy and graduated from the University of Mississippi in 1968 with a Bachelor of Science degree in Pharmacy. He immediately entered graduate school and received the Master's degree in Hospital Pharmacy in 1971. As a practicing pharmacist, Henry was Director of Pharmacy Operations at the Medical College of Virginia, a teaching complex of five hospitals in Richmond, Virginia. He then left the Medical College of Virginia to become Director of Professional Affairs for the United States Pharmacopeia in Washington, D.C., a post he held for five years.

The Southland beckoned and he went to Auburn, Alabama, in 1975 to become Assistant to the Dean and Assistant Professor of Pharmacy at Auburn University School of Pharmacy.

His speaking career began when he was called upon to speak on behalf of the United States Pharmacopeia, the book of official drug standards for the country. Since the book is about as exciting as a Chevrolet parts manual, he started making points using stories and anecdotes from his native land, the *Heart of Dixie.* His reputation as an after-dinner speaker spread nationwide, and he made the inevitable decision to become a full-time professional speaker, a decision implemented on January 1, 1978.

Robert Henry has spoken in 47 states including Alaska; he has also spoken in Canada and Puerto Rico. He is a very funny man who uses humor to take a penetrating look at contemporary problems. His down home stories will have you laughing uproariously when you hear them. Yet he skillfully conveys a message that will be long remembered.

You may contact Robert by writing to Robert H. Henry, 1419 East University Drive, Auburn, Alabama 36830 or by telephoning (205) 821-2415.

WIN WITH A.C.E.S.

by ROBERT H. HENRY

The fact that you're reading this book indicates that you're different. You're certainly not average. You might be considerably ahead of the pack. But, as good as you might be, have you given it your best shot? Are you so turned on that you're performing at 100% of your capacity?

Of course not. That's why you're reading this book. So let me begin by asking you a question. Why did you get up this morning? I usually get a nervous laugh in response to that question, but I'm deadly serious. If you can't think about it for a few minutes and give me a relatively thoughtful answer to the question, then I must ask you: Where are you going? What do you stand for? What do you believe in? What are your goals?

23

You've got to have goals, right? Wrong! I have traveled the length and width of this country telling people that you have to have goals. When doing this, I always let a strain come in my voice and roll my eyes toward the ceiling to impress the crowd with my sincerity. Then, just a few months ago, I saw a bumper sticker which said, "Goals Are for People Who Need Them." In a flash, I realized I had been wrong. You don't have to have goals—because you don't have to amount to anything. You can just exist. And, as nothing as you might become, you won't ever be totally worthless. You can always be a pitiful example.

I say it a little differently now. I say you've got to have goals—if you want to be a success. That's the truth.

Some successful people might appear to have gotten there without goals. Some people seem to have "lucked" their way to success. These apparently non-goaled success stories maybe didn't sit down and consciously go through a goal-setting process, but don't kid yourself— they had goals and that's why they made it.

There's a lovely story from *Alice in Wonderland*. Alice was walking one day and came to a fork in the road. She looked in a tree and saw a Cheshire Cat. She said, "Mr. Cheshire Cat, which road should I take?" He asked, "Where are you going?" She said, "I don't know." "Then," he answered, "it makes no difference which road you take."

If you don't know why you got up this morning, you might as well have stayed in bed—you'll get there just as quickly. But if you have goals, and if your goals are reasonable, practical, and obtainable, then you're well on the way to becoming the success you dreamed of being when you were 20 years old.

A lot of speakers talk about goals. I think some of them make a mistake in describing goals as a great, massive, ultimate objective.

I happen to believe that you can and must have many goals, from small to large. The one rule that must always apply is that the goal must be reasonable, practical, and obtainable—for *you*. Strive to do the best *you* can do, not to be as good or better than someone else.

I have a friend in Wharton, Texas, a fellow named Dr. James Blakely. In my opinion, "Doc" Blakely might very well be the funniest man in the world—at least of the ones I've heard. My aim (goal) as a platform humorist is not to be funnier or even as funny as my friend "Doc" Blakely. My goal at any specific speech is to be as funny as *I* can possibly be, given that situation, that audience, and the talents I have going for me.

If I set out, as some would suggest, to establish the one magnificent, encompassing goal toward which I'll strive, and I choose to be the Pope, I've got a problem. I don't care if this *is* the land of opportunity, I don't believe that a Southern Baptist from south Alabama has ever been made Pope. In fact, I'm comfortable in telling you that it won't happen for a long time.

If I choose to be Pope, I am doomed from the outset to failure, frustration, and disappointment. That goal is just not reasonable, practical, or obtainable for me.

Now I *can* become a Methodist. In fact, that's exactly what I did just a few months ago. For various reasons, I wanted to go to the Methodist Church. That goal was easily expressed, quite practical, and clearly obtainable. All I had to do was to drive one block farther on Sunday, walk in, sit down, and announce that I was the newest Methodist in Auburn, Alabama. For practical purposes, I had reached my goal.

It was quite exciting, actually. Since we have a friendly but spirited competition between the Methodist and Baptist churches, I was welcomed with open arms and hailed as an enlightened Christian by the Methodists, but some Baptists were heard to say they were glad the wild-eyed heretic had moved down the street. Oh well, it's commonly known that a Methodist is nothing but a Baptist who made good on his investments.

This is not to say you mustn't choose big goals. Certainly, you should go for the big ones and the bigger the better as long as they're reasonable, practical, and obtainable for you. I implore you to use your wildest imagination in choosing your goals. While I don't believe that absolutely anything that pops into your mind can be yours if you believe and work hard enough, I resolutely believe that only a few things will be denied you if you consciously define goals that are reasonable, practical, and obtainable.

If you don't understand a goal, it will be impossible for you to get there. If your goal is to be "great" some day, or to be a "success," or to make a "lot" of money, then it has no specific meaning. Your goals must be so well understood, so specific, and so simply expressed that you can write them down in two sentences or less.

And write them down you should. You can even express a goal as a picture. I have a friend who keeps a "wish" book on his desk. Upon entering business, his first wish (goal) was for a Cadillac. So he went to a Cadillac agency and got a picture of the exact car he wanted, along with the price. That picture went into his "wish" book where he could look at it every day. Nine months after he "pictured" his goal, it was parked in front of his office, paid for in full.

Very importantly, don't be frightened of what appears to be an impossible goal. If you spotted a particularly appealing apple on the topmost branch of a tree, you quite likely wouldn't try to leap into the air and pick off the apple in mid-flight. The reasonable and practical approach would be either to get a ladder or climb the tree, selecting one sturdy limb at a time to reach your goal.

A story is told of an expedition that crashed in the frozen wastelands of the Arctic. In a seemingly hopeless situation, facing a certain agonizing death if they stayed, the band of men headed for what they hoped would be civilization, 600 miles away.

When rescued, the men, all of whom survived, were interviewed by an incredulous press. The leader was asked, "How did you do it? How did you walk 600 miles through what may well be the most desolate, unforgiving, frozen terrain in the whole world?" He replied, "Oh, we didn't walk 600 miles. We walked one mile, 600 times."

Goals are dreams being acted upon. Faith without action is dead. Some confuse daydreams with goals. Not so!

Daydreams are harmless fantasies that lead you nowhere. They're not necessarily detrimental, but they can be. A Walter Mitty dream in which the dreamer always ends up a hero can be fun, and we all do this at one time or another.

However, a dream without action remains simply a dream with no form or substance. Until a dream is converted by action into a goal, those marvelous inner resources won't be mobilized that are necessary to propel one toward success. A crowd will follow a dreamer with a plan of action. On the other hand, the big dreamer who is content to pass from one dream to another soon loses the respect of his friends and ultimately his respect for himself.

In my family, we have a saying for the one who's always pursuing the big dream, always talking about what he's going to do, the big deals he'll pull off some day. When we hear these bigshot tales, someone in the family invariably rolls his eyes heavenward and says, "Gimme another drink of water."

This phrase comes from a story once told by comedian Dave Gardner in which two men went to work for a construction company on the same day. They were given shovels and told where to dig.

One man went to work with fervor, tearing into the soil as if his future depended upon the job he did that day. The other leaned heavily on his shovel, surveyed the construction site, and said, "Someday I'm gonna own me a company like this. I might even own this one. I'm gonna have me about 400 people on my payroll. I'll own 47 trucks, 14 tractors, and 3 Caterpillars. Gimme another drink of water."

Meanwhile, the other little fellow had fallen in love with his work. I mean he dug the diggin'. That shovel had become a part of his life.

Twenty years passed. The little fellow who diligently applied himself to his task on the first day is now president of the company, makes $100,000 a year, drives a Cadillac, and vacations in Europe.

The other fellow? He's still leaning on the shovel telling anyone who will listen that "Someday I'm gonna own this construction company. Gimme another drink of water."

The second step of goal setting, and equally important as the first, is to decide if you're willing to give up whatever you'll have to give up to reach your goal.

Would you like to make $100,000 next year? If the answer is yes, then go to any major university and sell grass. That's right. There's at least a $100,000 marijuana business each year at any major university in the country.

The second step is to decide if you're willing to give up what's necessary to achieve your $100,000 goal. Now friend, I'm tacky about jails. I don't like them. Never been in one and have no intention of going. I know that if I sell grass long enough, I'm gonna get caught and sent to jail. It was easy for me to decide that a $100,000 goal selling grass was not reasonable, practical, nor obtainable for me.

Let me tell you about one of my most personal and cherished goals. I have two little boys at home: Patrick, age 7, and Brent, age 4. I love those two little boys more than anything in the whole world. I love them so much my heart seems to ache sometimes when I look at them.

One of my goals is to be the best daddy I can possibly be. I read books about that. I study about that. I don't want to be a better daddy than one fellow or even as good as another. I just want to be the best daddy that I can possibly be.

This is a true story, and when I say it's true, it always is. Several months ago I had read far into the night. It was two o'clock in the morning when I started for bed. I went into my bedroom and there was a wife, two boys, and a dog in my bed. I thought to myself, "I ain't gonna get in that bed with a wife, two boys, and a dog." I went to the guest bedroom and went to bed alone.

About two thirty my little boy Patrick, a real daddy's boy, awakened and missed his daddy. As he will any night when I'm in that house, he began looking for me and I felt him slide in bed behind me and snuggle up real close. I lay on my side; my little boy raised up and kissed me on my shoulder and thinking he was speaking to a sleeping daddy spoke out loud, saying "I love you, Daddy."

Oh, I thought my heart would burst. I turned over and grabbed my little boy and kissed him a dozen times. I said, "Son, your Daddy loves you too. I love you more than anything in the whole world. Do you know how much I love you?" He said, "Yeah, Daddy, I sure do." I said, "Well, son, how do you know that?" He said, "Because you tell me every day."

How about you? When's the last time you told your children how much you love them? I don't care how old they are, you can't express your love too often or kiss them too much.

I can't keep my lips off my boys. My wife said "You're still kissing Patrick right on the mouth. That boy is seven years old. How long are you going to do that?" I said, "Until he's 35."

My little boys make my whole world turn around and, if God's willing, I'll enjoy telling them how much I love them every day until I die. That is a reasonable, practical, and obtainable goal for me.

A.C.E.S.

Now that you have your goals clearly in mind and so simply expressed that you can write them down in two sentences or less, I want you to think of a poker game. You understand poker. A handful of aces will win any poker game. I'm going to give you the aces to win the game you're playing. Your game might be far different from mine, but whatever the game, these aces will make a winner out of you.

A

A stands for *ambition.* Isn't that simple? Did I really need to tell you that? Of course you've got ambition; that's why you're reading this book. You want to be a success, to do a job well, to be better this year than you were last.

One of the greatest stories I ever heard regarding ambition, the will to succeed, concerns Pete Strudwick, a 47-year-old Californian whose ambition was to be a marathon runner. Do you know how far a marathon is?

Twenty-six miles, 385 yards. This 47-year-old man has run over 30 marathons, including the Boston Marathon—and he has no feet. No feet! He runs on stumps. Someone asked him, "Pete, how do you run 26 miles with no feet?" He replied, "You don't lean backwards." Isn't that fantastic? What a marvelous plan for achieving any goal. Set your goal and don't lean backwards.

A also stands for *attitude.* What a marvelous ace to have up your sleeve. The magic of believing in yourself will make a loser into a winner. Oh, the excitement that comes with self-confidence—knowing that you've got the goods and chasing that opportunity to deliver. Be an optimist:

> *Twixt optimist and pessimist*
> *The difference is quite droll.*
> *The optimist the donut sees,*
> *The pessimist the hole.*

Are you looking at a donut, or staring at a hole? It's up to you, they're *your* eyes.

I believe with all my heart that you can consciously choose to be successful. You can choose to be happy. You can choose to be enthusiastic. You can choose to make a lot of money.

Every morning when I get up with my boys, I tell them what a terrific day it's going to be. I begin the day by telling them that something good will happen to them this day. Of course, they always want to know what good thing will happen and I never know. So I tell them to write it down when it happens and we'll discuss it that night. Sure enough, every night my boys can tell me of at least one good thing that happened during the day. And each day I have no doubt that they'll have something to report because they leave home expecting something good to happen.

31

Before you leave your bedroom each morning, I recommend that you stand in front of the mirror, throw out your chest, give yourself a big smile and say, "Friend, you look terrific. You are a 100% winner. There's greatness in you just waiting to leap out. Something good is going to happen to you today."

Now the first few times you do this you're going to feel awfully silly. Your spouse is sure to crack up laughing if he or she is in earshot. The kids will think that mom or dad has finally bought the farm. But friend, if you'll force yourself to do this for ten days, you'll be amazed at the results. You will have programmed yourself for a winning attitude.

The people with whom you associate have a terrific influence on your attitude. There are a lot of people out there just waiting to whittle you down to their size. Even more insidious are the good friends who don't realize how negative they are. Some people, believe it or not, will resent your appearance of being on top of the world and jump at every opportunity to knock you off. Don't you let them do it.

If anybody tries to put you down, to diminish your value, to make you less than you have a right to be, you avoid them like the plague. Don't let anybody intimidate you and make you deal from an inferior position. You can only be diminished or intimidated if you consciously give someone permission to do so. I give no person that permission and I'm asking you to do the same.

A change in attitude can occur with a snap of a finger, as if a light were turned on. And just as quickly, the change in attitude can effect a change in your life style.

An often-told and beautiful story concerns coach Lou Little, who coached at Georgetown University before he became famous at Columbia.

Coach Little had a tackle on his team who really wasn't much of a football player. He had never played more than a few minutes in a game in the four years he had been on the team. Even as a senior he only got in a game in the last few minutes, and then only if Georgetown was ahead 20 or 30 points.

One week before the last game of the season and the final game of the lad's football career, the boy's father died. He went home to be with his mother and bury his father.

On Wednesday before the game Coach Little called the boy at his home and said, "Son, you don't need to come back for the game this weekend. You stay with your mother, that's where you belong. We'll get along without you on Saturday."

On the day of the game, as the team dressed in the locker room, Coach Little looked up to see the boy walk in the door. He went to him and said, "Son, I don't understand. I told you we'd handle things. You didn't need to come back." He said, "Coach, this is the big game of the year. If you need me I want to be here."

Coach Little was touched and impressed by the boy's attitude. When the team went to the field to warm up, the boy went to the coach and said, "I want to ask a special favor. I want to start the game today."

Coach Little was surprised. This boy had never started a college football game but he was impressed with his determination. Also, there was something different about him today. He said, "All right, son, I'll let you start your final game, but I might have to take you out after a few minutes."

With the kick of the first ball, the boy played like a man possessed. For 60 minutes he never came out of the game. He was driving, slashing, hitting, tackling—everybody's All-American.

33

After the game, Coach Little went to him and asked, "Son, how did you do it? Why, I never saw a man play football like you did today. You were everyone's outstanding player of the game. How did you do it?"

He replied, "Coach, you never met my daddy, did you?"

Coach Little said, "No, son, I never had that pleasure."

The boy said, "Did you ever see me walking arm in arm with my daddy across the campus?"

Coach Little said, "Yes, I saw that a number of times."

"Not many people knew my daddy was blind. Today was the first game my daddy ever saw me play. I played today for my daddy."

A mediocre football player changed his attitude and became an All-American. A change of attitude can do the same for you. Your whole life can be changed in the instant it takes to change your attitude.

C

C stands for *commitment*. Are you committed to your goals? Are you willing to take a stand for what you believe in? Surprisingly enough, most folks are not committed to much of anything at all. If you suddenly speak out and show a strong commitment on a subject, you probably will be surprised at the people who will follow your lead.

If your goal is reasonable, practical, and obtainable, and if you commit yourself to it to such an extent that nothing is allowed to turn your head, you'll wind up in the winner's circle.

One advantage to a careful analysis of your goals in the beginning is that there must be no room for a second or third best showing. You should generate a passion for success and a hatred of failure. Where your goals are concerned don't ever be a "good" loser. If you can pat yourself on the back and be satisfied with less than your best, then your goal was too high to begin with.

Please understand, failure in one or more endeavors does not mean that you're a loser. The world doesn't come to an end because you fail at something. The important thing is to get up when you've been knocked down and try again. No man was ever beaten by being knocked down. A man is beaten because he doesn't get up.

Most successful men have been beaten a few times, and some many times, before they realized great success. But a common thread bound them together: they committed themselves to succeed and they passionately hated their failures.

I have a dear friend named Fred Alias who's a big shot executive in the hotel-motel business. Freddie taught me a valuable lesson—never look back. No matter how bad your failure, no matter how tragic, foolish, or humiliating, learn from it, certainly, but never, never, never, look back. It's gone, done, over. If you dwell on your past failures, you'll never progress to your future successes.

Friend, I consider myself a successful man. I've got everything that most people feel a successful man should have. But it hasn't always been this way. I've been down on my knees with the tears streaming down my face saying, "Lord, how in the world did I ever get myself in this mess?" I felt that the Lord said something like, "Robert, get up off your knees. You can't win an argument, a battle, or another man's respect by looking up at him. You gotta look him straight in the eye." I got up and I haven't been down since.

Art Holst is a National Football League official and one of the greatest humorous-motivational speakers I've ever heard. I heard him tell this story and I don't believe I'll ever hear a better illustration of what commitment can do for a person who has set what some might consider an impossible goal.

About 35 years ago, a boy was born with one half of a right foot and only a stump where his right arm should have been. That boy got to high school and he wanted to play football. He went to his mother and said "Mother, I want to play football." She said, "No, son, that's a rough, tough game. Those are big, mean boys. They'll hurt you." He said, "Mother, I've got to play football," and he committed himself to that goal. He played high school football.

When that boy got to college he wanted to be the best college football player that he could possibly be. He committed himself to that goal—and he was.

Finally, that fellow wanted to be a professional football player more than anything in the whole world. He totally committed everything he had going for him to that goal.

Seven years ago that man stood in Sugar Bowl Stadium in New Orleans, Louisiana. Eighty-six thousand people were nearly hysterical. Seventeen seconds were left on the clock. The score was 17 to 15 in favor of his opponents. That poor, disadvantaged, crippled man stood before the ball and hardly a sound was heard except his foot connecting with the ball and it went 63 yards, split the goal post and he won the game. With that kick, Tommy Dempsey kicked his way into professional football's Hall of Fame.

Did he kick it with the good foot? No, as a matter of fact, he didn't. He kicked it with the bummer. He was committed to being the best and he's in the record book to prove it.

C also stands for *communication*. Do you realize

that we don't communicate in this country anymore? Either we don't talk at all, or we fail to express our ideas adequately, or the words and phrases we understand so well have a different meaning to the person or persons with whom we are trying to communicate.

Communication often breaks down at the family level. A man comes home from a hard day at the office completely drained, feeling very sorry for himself, and probably thinking only of himself. He takes one giant step inside and what's the first thing he hears from the little lady? "Get these kids away from me! They're driving me crazy!" Of course, he replies, "Whaddaya think I've been doing all day, twiddling my thumbs?" And the argument is on.

Or maybe the happy family has settled down for the evening's television and she announces "The car is on fire!" He calmly replies, "We'll talk about it during the commercial."

Hey daddy—or mother—when's the last time you asked your teenager to sit down for a talk? Or do you ever listen to your teenager? I guess the better question is can you sit in the same room with your teenager and carry on a civilized conversation without beginning to shout, or argue, or put down his or her beliefs? I wonder if the drug problem would be such a problem if those teenagers could have come to their parents and said "Hey, mom and dad, I've got a problem. I hurt inside. Can I talk to you?"

Words sometime get in the way of communication. I like the story about John Lovelace, who, at the age of 83 and nearly deaf, got a new hearing aid. He bragged to his friend L.T. Tucker, saying, "L.T., I've got the finest hearing aid money can buy. Why, I can hear the birds sing 100 yards away. I can hear the autumn leaves rustled by a gentle breeze. I can hear a squirrel walking through the limbs of a tree." L.T. said, "Mr. John, that's wonderful.

What kind is it?" John Lovelace said, "Aw, it's about a quarter till three."

E

E stands for *enthusiasm*. Do you have enthusiasm in your life and do you let it shine through like a beacon?

Enthusiasm in a person will attract people quicker than any other quality. People like to be around winners, and an enthusiastic person is immediately identified as a winner.

Enthusiastic people don't burden others with their problems. Never, ever presume to unload your problems on someone else. Eighty per cent of the people don't care and the other twenty per cent will use them against you.

Have you ever known a real hypochondriac? Do you recall how happy they seemed when you agreed to listen to their list of health problems? Their problems might have been a bit interesting when you first heard them but oh, how boring they become. Do you remember when you first began to dread a visit by your hypochondriac friend and began to devise methods to avoid him or her?

The same treatment is in store for people who persist in relating other types of problems.

I have a standard reply for those who ask how I am: Terrific. I don't care if I have a fever, headache, and just had to turn down three speeches because of prior commitments, the reply is the same: Terrific.

I encourage you to try this approach. You'll be surprised at how people respond. Too often people seem to expect an unenthusiastic answer with a mention of the most current problem. When you answer "terrific," you will actually brighten their day and make them a little happier.

Remember when I talked about attitude and I said I

believed you could consciously choose to be happy? Well, you can consciously choose to be enthusiastic, too.

I gave you some exercises to go through in front of the mirror to boost your attitude about yourself. As long as you're there and have already made a complete fool out of yourself, you might as well work on your enthusiasm at the same time. You should force yourself to bounce out of bed in the morning and shout, "I feel great. I feel terrific. This is going to be a wonderful day." In the beginning you're going to feel awfully silly and your family will probably laugh their heads off. In addition, unless you're used to this sort of thing, you're going to feel just the opposite to what you're shouting. That's why I say you must *force* yourself to do it. But, if you will go through this ritual for ten days, you won't have to force yourself any more. You will honestly feel the exciting enthusiasm with which you've programmed yourself.

I'm probably the happiest fellow I know. I've got everything in the world going for me. I've got those two little boys who make my whole world turn around. I've been married to a gorgeous lady for 15 years who could be Mrs. America any year. I make a heckuva lot of money. I travel all over the United States doing exactly what I'd rather do more than anything else in the world. Everything's going great for me and I ain't gonna let anybody mess that up.

How about you? Do you like what you're doing so much that you'd do it for nothing if you had to? Or, do you, like so many people I meet, dislike your life and work so much that it's turned you into a bitter, disillusioned, unhappy, disappointed person? If this is the case, get the hell out. I don't care if you're 65 years old and have been on the job for 40 years. If you hate it, walk off and leave it. You, and the job, will be better off after the decision.

But if you have enthusiasm and if you'll let it shine through like a beautiful beacon, attracting those who share, or would like to share your zest for life, you're destined to be a winner and nobody can stop you.

Ira Hayes, a great professional speaker and "Mr. Enthusiasm" of the American platform, has a great definition for enthusiasm. Ira says "enthusiasm is a bridegroom on his wedding night who goes to the wall switch to turn off the lights—and he's in bed before the room gets dark."

S

S stands for *service*. Service to your colleagues. Service to your community. Service without a price tag. Anonymous service is the best of all. Most importantly, service to your God. Give back to Him some of the magnificent gifts He has so bountifully given to you.

Friend, know the incredible joy, the excitement, the thrill of taking all your problems, burdens, responsibilities and laying them right over in the hands of God. Of course, you've got to have faith. Surely I didn't need to tell you that.

But don't have faith like the fellow who fell from the mountain top and caught onto a small tree, which was the only thing that kept him from the valley floor 2,000 feet below. He called out, "Help! Somebody up there help me!" A voice came to him saying, "Yes, I'll help you." The fellow said, "Who is that up there?" The voice said, "It's me, the Lord. Turn loose the tree." After a long pause, the fellow called out, "Is anybody else up there?"

I've given you my secrets, the A.C.E.S. that will take you to the mountain top. They aren't secrets at all, since so many of us talk about them. But if I can be an example to you and show you how I've used them to be a winner, then I have accomplished my purpose.

MARK VICTOR HANSEN

Mark Victor Hansen conducts seminars and lectures for business and professional people throughout the United States. He speaks annually to hundreds of thousands.

Mark was educated at Southern Illinois University where he did his graduate work in Design Science and Health. While there, he was a student ambassador to India and Vietnam and a research assistant to Dr. R. Buckminster Fuller.

Mark was vice president of marketing of a New York based company where he tripled their sales growth within two years. After achieving *his* goal he has evolved into a professional speaker and sales trainer, sharing the formulas for success with others. Mark is co-author of *Stand Up, Speak Out and Win!*—one of the best selling books on attitude improvement.

He created and produced several educational and inspirational sets of cassette tapes that have enhanced hundreds of thousands of peoples' sales abilities, self-confidence and self-image. He has shared the lecture platform with Bob Richards, Earl Nightingale, Zig Ziglar, Cavett Robert, Chris Hegarty, and many of America's top speakers.

The topics Mark dramatically presents include: "Celebrating You!" "Seven Steps to a Positive Self-Image!" "Unlimited Prospects (Business) Right Here & Right Now," "How to Outperform Yourself," "The Ten Commandments of Ideas," and "Management by Action."

Mark Victor Hansen is currently finishing his doctorate in Mind Science.

You may contact Mark by writing to Mark Victor Hansen Associates, 117-F Riverside Drive, Newport Beach, California 92663 or telephoning (714) 759-9304.

CELEBRATING YOU: THE TEN COMMANDMENTS OF IDEAS

by MARK VICTOR HANSEN

The human mind is a very interesting, very powerful tool. In this chapter, I'm going to talk about how you can always make it work positively and productively. I'm going to talk about positive self-image. I'm going to suggest that, with a positive self-image, many of you could make more money than you've ever made before. How can you develop a positive self-image? By understanding the ten commandments of ideas.

First Commandment

The first commandment says, "It's normal and natural for adults to have approximately a thousand ideas a day, plus or minus a few." Now a lot of those ideas are what we call low-grade ideas: I've got to go to the bathroom, I forgot to tell my husband I won't be home for dinner, I forgot to have the kids brush their teeth, I ought to have the car serviced next week, etc. From this pool of a thousand ideas and thoughts, approximately fifty are going to be productive, life-benefitting, and potentially profitable. The first commandment of ideas tells you, in three points, how to manage your ideas.

1. *Write them down.* Point one of the first commandment tells you that ideas are useless unless you write them down. Everybody has more ideas than they can use. Most ideas flit through your head as inspiration, thought-form, flash, intuition, or hunch. If you don't write them down, they'll disappear as quickly as they came. I keep a little diary, called *Mark's Sunshine Idea Book,* just for that purpose.

Once you start writing down your intuitions and flashes, some interesting things happen. When you write down a major, big idea, a lot of times a little idea will follow and it'll tell you how to pull off the big idea. If you're really on purpose and you're really dedicated to high achievement during the goal-setting period, you're going to have ideas come to you in the middle of the night. Have you ever awakened in the middle of the night with an idea? Have you ever bothered enough to open your eyes and write it down on a piece of paper you keep next to your bed? Few people bother. The point I'm making: You should always carry with you a little white card or notebook so you can just write down the idea. Just the idea. All riches and achievement have their beginning in the idea. All the recognition you'll ever get starts with the idea.

It's also important that you write down every one of your goals in life. I've got about fifty pages of goals. When you write them down, they start taking on pictures. What you picture is what you get, and once you can picture your goals, they get easier and easier to obtain, and you reach them sooner and sooner.

The human mind works when it's used; it doesn't work when it's not used.

2. *Review what you've written.* The second point of the first commandment tells you: Once you make the habit of recording what your mind tells you, you've regularly got to review what you've written. You've got to review your goals first thing in the morning and then the last thing at night before you go to sleep. I want to give some examples of that.

Bruce Jenner, the decathlon winner at the Montreal Olympics, was recently interviewed. The interviewer asked, "Bruce, have you always been a big-time winner?"

Jenner replied, "Man, no way. I was the most abjected, rejected, dejected Olympian America has ever sent anywhere, at any time, for any reason." He continued, "I was in Munich. I failed miserably. I lost every one of the events. I went to bed that night with tears in my eyes. I woke up about 3 o'clock still just crying my heart out, and walked the streets of Munich until six A.M. At six A.M. the newspapers hit the stands and they had a picture of the guys who had won the gold, bronze, and silver medals. I cut out the picture of the person who had won the gold medal. I put my face where his face was, edited out his scores, and added in my scores that I would win in Montreal four years later. I took that sheet of paper and I put it over my bed, and it was the first thing I looked at for twenty minutes in the morning and the last thing I cogitated, ruminated, and meditated on before I went to sleep at night."

See, that's regular reviewing.

Jenner concluded, "I won the Montreal Olympics four years before they held them because I had it in my mind."

Everything starts in the human mind, which we'll go into shortly.

3. *Take action now.* The third point of the first commandment is that you've got to take action now—that's the old *do-it-now* formula. One of my friends is a great salesman. At one time he was earning $30,000 a year, he'd just been divorced, his wife wanted an extraordinary settlement, he wanted to stop selling. I said, "My friend, instead, put yourself in an action pattern and decide to expand your income up to what you want." The guy started making more money than he'd ever made before. He expanded his income to $80,000 a year, selling scientific products. The same success story can happen to you, male or female, it doesn't matter, when you get on purpose about yourself. The guy went and made all that money, got a magnificent house for himself, invited us over for a champagne party. Incidentally, life treats you just like you treat life, so if you're good to yourself, life's good to you. And whatever you're ready for is ready for you. It's a very curious phenomenon. It's just like Delta Airlines' ad, "Delta is ready when you are!" Success is ready when you are, because success is an inside job, it's a mental job.

I went over to see his new house. I walked in and immediately saw that the house was equal to *my* self-image. I walked in and said, "My friend, this place is for me! It is absolutely equal to my self-image. I'm going to positively hex your house."

He said, "Come on, man, I just moved in here, what are you doing?"

I said, "No, this place is just perfect, it's got the right

number of fireplaces, the right number of bedrooms, three inches of carpet—upstairs, downstairs, basement, everything's perfect, everything that I want."

He said, "Come on, man, don't do that to me, I just moved in."

I said, "Look, I'm not being malicious or coercive but I see myself in this house."

You see, that's the law of mind. When you start saying, "That's for me," you've got it already. Every reader, pick whatever it is you want, whatever good thing you desire, and say, "That's for me." When you say that, your pupils will probably dilate. Why? Because what you get in your heart or in your deeper, innermost, highermost subconscious mind must inevitably manifest itself, which we'll talk about in just a second.

Well, to make a long story very short, I am now living in that house and my friend has moved into another great home in another state. That's evolution for both of us. That house was one of the goals I wrote down. Anything you desire will come to manifest itself if you write it down because writing it down brings you to a point in consciousness where it's yours already. You see, first of all you've got to claim the good that you desire in consciousness. For example, when I go to a speaking engagement, I arrive mentally before I arrive physically. I expect a good, great, grand, and terrific audience, and I almost always have one. See how easy it is? Whatever thought vibes you send out to your projects, if you expect them to be great they come out great. If you say, "Oh, no, I don't know if it's going to work," sure enough it fails.

Second Commandment

The second commandment says, "You serve your ideas and then your ideas serve you." You see, whatever you lift up into your mind's eye you become. Earl Nightingale says it so elegantly that it bears repetition: "You become what you think about." The Bible says, "As people think-eth in their heart so are they." As a man or woman thinks in his or her deeper, innermost, highermost subconscious mind, that's what he or she becomes. If you believe you're only going to be mildly successful, then that's all you'll be.

Think about fish in an aquarium. Do you know that fish grow to the size of their aquarium? If you get a bigger aquarium, you get bigger fish. What am I saying? I'm saying that you must stretch your thinking to fit the goal you've written down. Remember that you are somebody special. Everybody, you know, when things go wrong, wants to blame someone else. What you should do when things go wrong is point to yourself and say, *"I'm* some-body special!" And you *are.* Then you should change things to go right.

To follow commandment number two, serve your ideas and then your ideas serve you, you must know what ideas you serve. Most people don't know what ideas they serve. So many individuals come up to me and they say, "Mark, don't you ever get depressed?" And I say, "Nope, never." And they say, "How depressing." They are serving the idea that depression is acceptable to them. The sec-ond commandment goes on to say that you've got to have a definite, positive, specific idea held constant in con-sciousness, and inevitably it must manifest itself often in ways beyond our understanding. For a long time Mu-hammed Ali was in fact the greatest. When I was nine years old and delivering newspapers, his face graced the Chicago *Tribune* and the caption beneath said, "I am the greatest." It didn't say, "I'm a half the greatest, I'm a quar-ter the greatest, or maybe tomorrow I'll be the greatest." He served the idea that he *was* the greatest. Now

Muhammed Ali has lost three fights in his life. With the first two he lost, he had said beforehand, *"If* I win." You see, none of us can be half-hearted and succeed. You can't doubt even one percent, as we saw in the movie *Rocky*. You've got to be one hundred percent for yourself. You've got to say, "I'm a big-time winner right here and right now." It's got to be definite, positive, and specific. Ali lost his third fight, and his championship, to Leon Spinks. And the beautiful thing is that his best student, Leon Spinks, says, "That's true, Ali's the greatest but I'm the best." He won't take anything from Ali. Now the point about Ali's third loss is that he wasn't specific beforehand. He never said, "I'm going to K.O. you in the third round." He forgot to get specific. When you and I set our goals, they have *got* to be specific, so we know exactly what we are serving.

What do you want? We're going to talk about that shortly. It is critical. What you've got to do with your Sunshine Idea Book is write down what you want. Somebody can say, "Well, when are we going to get what we want?" First of all, you've got to know what you want before you can pick when you're going to get it. Your Sunshine Idea Book is a what-to-do book rather than a when-to-do book, although when to do it—goal-getting—is an important part of goal-setting. Writing down a specific idea to serve is simple. But that idea has got to be definite, it's got to be specific, it's got to be positive, or you'll be serving the wrong thing. Negative goals are just as easy to reach as positive goals, but positive goals are a whole lot more fun.

When you set goals, you've got to set them in six ways. You should get a piece of paper and, as you read, write down what you're going to give yourself in each of these six categories.

1. *What are you going to give yourself mentally?* Most of us know how to eat food three times a day, but how often do we feed our minds? I'm talking about positive, good stuff. We eat physically three times a day, and we ought to eat mentally three times a day. We ought to put in inspirational, motivational, educational stuff three times a day.

2. *What are you doing physically for yourself?* Are you exercising every day ritualistically and systematically? I hope you pick a mentor, somebody that you really want to emulate, which means to try to match and surpass. Now we all learn one of four ways. We learn by *identification, instruction, example,* and *imitation.* Interesting. Those are the only four ways you learn. To learn by imitation, you must pick good models, because you're going to copy the behavior of the people you hang out with. Pick somebody that's better than you are. If you play tennis for exercise, you know that you should play with somebody better than you are, or you won't improve. If you want to improve your game, you must play with someone you can identify with, who can instruct you, who can serve as your example, and whom you can imitate. My guru in motivation is seventy-two years young, a bountifully beautiful, mature individual who is effervescent and jolly—the most professional human being in the whole world. I just love him. He's got a poem I want to share with you. It fits here:

> *He was such a very cautious lad,*
> *He never romped or played,*
> *He never smoked, he never drank,*
> *He never even kissed a maid,*
> *So when he up and passed away*
> *Insurance was denied.*

They claimed because he never really lived,
He never really died.

—Cavett Robert

Be certain *you* don't die before you're dead. Exercise every day. Do calisthenics, yoga, jogging, or rope jumping, and constantly build up your capacity.

3. *What are your family goals?* We're talking about high-quality time between husbands and wives. A great study was just done by my friend, Chris Hegarty, with six, seven, and eight-year-olds. He interviewed many children. He asked, "Would you prefer to spend time with Dad or the television set?" And Dad came in a close second. It's an important kind of concept. We'd better be spending high-quality time in the family, with both spouses and each child, at least once a week, doing what he or she wants to do.

4. *What is your financial goal?* This one's fun. This has got three parts to it:

A. *What do you want to earn this year?* This is a boom year, there's never recession or depression out in the world—it's always in your mind. If you're a little negative, you're too negative, and you're going to get hardening of the attitudes. You're either enjoying ascent or descent based on your own mental experience. And you choose your mental experience. It's such a powerful thing. Most people don't know what experience they're picking. So many people come up to me and say, "I'm catching hell all the time." I say, "Well, put your mitt down!"

After you decide upon your annual goal, break it down into months, then weeks, then into *do-able* days and hours. For example, if you're in sales, do 10% better every month than the month before. To achieve the

10%, you'll probably only have to close one extra sale per month. Go linearly onward and upward.

B. *What are you going to save?* There's a book I highly recommend called *The Richest Man in Babylon.* The book says, "Part of all I earn is mine to keep." It also says, "Save ten percent of everything you earn. Pay yourself first, *then* pay everybody else."

C. *What investments are you going to make?* You should particularly invest in yourself by improving yourself. You should read more than you ever read before. I read at least a book a day. If you're not reading a book a month, you're getting behind. You should put more good stuff inside yourself than you've ever done before. Houdini said getting a rabbit out of the hat isn't any trick, it's getting him in there in the first place. Getting success out of a businessperson isn't any trick, it's getting the inspiration in there in the first place. As a favor to yourself, spend the first fifteen or twenty minutes every morning reading some self-help action book. Get up just that extra bit early before the kids even get out, because if your attitude's good you send those kids out with a good attitude, and they're going to make the teacher's attitude better.

The average income in America is almost $10,000 annually. Compounded by 45 work years, that's almost $500,000. When you decide to *invest* in something, let's say income-producing real estate, buying one house or apartment per year, you'll ultimately become rich.

5. *What are you giving yourself socially?* What I'm encouraging you to do is give yourself a vacation that you've never given yourself before. Where is it that you want to go? Write it down. And write down *when* you're going to take yourself there. The law of mind is that you

only get what you give yourself. You should think of the law of the mind in the first person: *"I'm* giving myself all the best."

Most importantly, ask yourself, "Who am I associating with?" Consider who your best friends are. Are they encouraging you socially, financially, emotionally, physically, and/or spiritually? If they're not bringing you up, cut them loose. Eleanor Roosevelt said, "No one can hurt me unless I give them my permission."

6. *What are you doing spiritually?* I don't care what church, temple, or synagogue you go to, but if you take your kids and stay with them fifty times by the time they hit age twelve, there's a ninety-eight percent less chance of alcoholism, criminality, and drug abuse because spirituality, like self-confidence, has got to be caught, it can't be taught. If you don't stay with your children in church, they say, "Oh, Mom and Dad, ha ha, they didn't think this was very important. Dad doesn't think the minister, priest, or rabbi is going to hit him with anything important so he split. When I grow up I'm not going to church. He forced me." It is critical, very subliminal but critical, that you provide your children with a good impression, just like you should find a good model for yourself.

Third Commandment

Commandment number three says, "Everything starts with an idea." This is why you must write down specific ideas and know what ideas you are serving. All riches and all achievement had their beginning in an idea. When you've got an idea, you've got everything that you need. All you've got to do is maintain that idea steadfastly and not procrastinate. And the way you end procrastination is just make a decision. Most people come up to me and say, "Well, Mark, I'm going to stop procrastinating tomorrow." It won't work. Gonna-doers are never-doers. They're gonna begin to commence to start tomorrow. You've got to start right here and right now. This commandment also says that ideas are the birthplace of all art. Pick an artist like Norman Rockwell or Andy Wyeth. It is just spectacular what they see in their mind's eye. You see, success is an inside job. It's inside out. What are you harvesting and harboring in your mind?

All music starts with an idea. Several years ago, a twenty-seven-year-old musician set his lifetime goal upon having a gold record. He spent two years preparing the music. He also had a handicap that most people don't have. He was blind. He worked thirty-six hours at a time. He never saw it get dark outside and he wouldn't allow anyone to tell him the time. He produced his gold record. His name is Stevie Wonder. He had one idea, he pedestalized it, he lifted it up in his consciousness, it consumed him, and it benefits all of us by giving us the kind of music that we desire to hear.

Architecture begins with an idea. If you want to uplift your mind, visit all the great estates in the country. All over the country there are estates that are examples of beauty, grandeur, excellence, and poshness, environments that bring out the best in you. Some of the architecture I hope you'll visit is Frank Lloyd Wright's. It is just magnificent. When I was in Tulsa recently, some friends took me at dusk to Oral Roberts University. Most of it is made out of gold-colored material, and I've never seen something shimmering at dusk so beautifully. Every kid on the campus, male or female, said hello to me. It was the nicest, warmest, friendliest campus I'd ever been on, and I'm sure I've been on two hundred of the two thousand university and college campuses in America. I said, "Boy, you can feel the presence of God here." Art in any form brings Him closer, and inspires those in its presence.

Let me talk about a book I highly recommend: *Think and Grow Rich*. It's a powerful book. Three of the top sales people in the world read that book and have pedestalized it as their sales bible. In that book, Napoleon Hill wrote a key line that said, "Anything the mind can conceive and believe it can achieve." Now one salesman last year outsold fifteen hundred of the eighteen hundred insurance companies. A top car salesman read it, came to understand it, and last year sold eighteen hundred cars and twelve hundred trucks. One of the top real estate sales people is only twenty-seven, and he sold five houses a day last year, all because of his attitude. He conceived that he'd sell each house. He got so on purpose with the idea that it consumed him. He did it, and he still has lots and lots of time for his family and leads a good, positive life. Success in life deals with the commandment we're covering. Everything starts with ideas, with basic principles, like what goes up must come down. It doesn't matter whether you're male or female, black, white, educated, uneducated, handsome, ugly. Principles are no respecters of individuals. They just work for anyone who works with them. When you put an idea to work, it is going to work. It works whether it's in any one of the disciplines, art, or sales. It's going to work every time.

This commandment goes on to say, "Ideas are the creative, causative stuff of conscience." What does that mean? It means that you are responsible for your every idle word. Have you ever walked into somebody's house and had them say, "I'll never get this mess cleaned up! Please forgive me"? What they're doing is bad mouthing their own environment, and it never gets cleaned up. Business people say, "I can never make this company work," and all they're doing is sending out the wrong mental vibrations. It doesn't cost you any more to say positive things.

This commandment says, "Thoughts are things. When considered, believed, and acted upon, they cause effects and results." Therefore, whatever ideas you energize, you will realize and realize and realize.

Let's go back to Napoleon Hill, who said, "Anything the mind can conceive and believe it can achieve." Critical idea. A top salesman, Joe Gandolfo, carved that motto into a thousand dollar walnut desk and put a glass top over it. Jules Verne said something similar: "Anything one mind can conceive other minds can achieve." Von Braun read Verne's idea and said, "I'm going to talk to John F. Kennedy." He went to Kennedy and said, "We're going to land a man on the moon." Kennedy said, "It's a great idea, let's do it in ten years." We did it in nine years and two months. It doesn't matter what or how big your goal, you've got to reach, you've got to stretch to get there. If you've got a little goal that you know you'll accomplish, you won't do anything with it. The goal's got to be just slightly bigger than your grasp. In my talks, I often ask members of the audience to walk over to a wall and reach as high as they think they can. After they have stretched as far as they can, I ask them to reach higher. And they can always go a few more inches. What's the point? It's the little difference that's all the difference. You know, water is hot at two hundred eleven degrees. At two hundred twelve degrees, you've suddenly got boiling water—steam power, which in Colorado will raise a hundred-thousand-pound locomotive up the highest hill of the tallest peak. That one degree difference is all the difference. It's that little extra that does all the extra.

Fourth Commandment

The fourth commandment says, "Ideas can and will solve all problems." There is no problem bigger than you. There can't be. The problem is nothing more than an idea when you look at it appropriately and correctly. Therefore, there are always ways to solve a problem. A book that was a lot of fun for me to read is called *The Very, Very Rich*, by Max Gunther. Gunther said that the beautiful thing about all the very rich, while we don't applaud them very much, is that they always find a way to solve any problem. If you're confronted with a mountain, you'll either go through it, under it, above it, or around it if your gold mine's on the other side. My guru says obstacles are those things that get in your way when you're not focused on your goal clearly enough. As long as you've got a clear mental picture of where you're going and what you want, you're home free. It says the only crisis or lack that ever exists is in the need of a good positive workable solution or idea. In 1974 when the Arabs pulled an embargo on us and interest rates just went skyrocketing up to 18%, I lost fifty thousand dollars overnight. One day the bank called me up and said, "You got two million dollars worth of contracts, interest rate is 18%, ha ha, you're out of business." The banker was slipping me a lot of mental static. And for six months I accepted that until I learned some of the things I'm writing in this chapter. When you want to solve a problem you've got to go a little deeper into the recesses of your consciousness because the solution is waiting. All of us have at least eighteen billion totally available and probably underused brain cells. But what happens when things go wrong is that most of us look at our little inabilities rather than our vast, bountiful, and omni-expanding abilities.

Commandment number four also says that a problem must be viewed as a challenge, growth opportunity, exciting circumstance, situation, experiment, or experience. Norman Vincent Peale once put a call through to W. Clement Stone and said, "We've got a problem." Stone replied, "Ridiculous!" Peale said, "But you don't understand, we've got a double bad problem!" Stone shouted, "Then that's double good." A positive attitude opens your mind and makes it receptive to good positive ideas that'll work in the here and now. If you say, "Oh no, I've got a bad problem that's on top of me," you've handicapped yourself by consenting to the burden of the problem. All you have to do is say, "I'm on top of my situation."

There are two positive ways to solve a problem. Number one is to prevent it. If you're looking forward, usually you can prevent it. Most problems repeat themselves. If you're running out of money, all you have to do is quit thinking negative, poor thoughts and start thinking positive, rich thoughts. The human mind can't hold a poverty thought and a prosperity thought at the same time. You can't say something negative when you're smiling. You can't say, "I'm rich and I can't afford it." You can't deny what you affirm. In other words, if you say, "I'm rich" but subconsciously say, "I can't pay for the new muffler," when someone comes up to you and complains of not being able to afford something, you'll say, "I know just how you feel." The state of fear is picked up faster than anything else because ninety-nine percent of the people spend ninety-nine percent of their time in a state of fear. You can benefit everybody else when you decide to be self-confident and decide to be on purpose in life. You see, you help more people get up by being up yourself. If you're down, you drag other people down. When somebody calls you on the telephone and you say, "Well, how's everything?" and he or she says, "Didn't you hear?" and begins telling you about something negative, like illness or divorce, either you turn that conversation around or you say, "Oh, I forgot, I have something to do and I've got to get to it. I apologize. I'll call you later." And hang up. Don't listen to anybody bad mouth anything. Don't listen to stories about car accidents, death, or illness. Whatever it is, you don't care and you don't want to hear about it. A girlfriend recently asked me if I wanted to hear about a couple's divorce. I said, "Ask me if I'm interested." So she asked, "Are you interested?" I said, "No. Will it benefit me or him or her if I know about the divorce?" She said, "No." I said, "Well, then, I don't want to hear about it." I did a seminar for a group of married women recently. I asked, "Do you spend most of your time thinking about divorce and separation or love and romance?" Ninety-nine percent said, "Divorce and separation." I said, "That's why we've got sixty percent of you getting divorced." Whatever you think about comes into your experience. If you say, "So and so got divorced," *you're* en route to divorce. So get it out of your mind.

People may say you're not normal if you don't want to hear negative stories. But there's never been a successful person who's not slightly warped. It's normal to be blah and have a case of the blahs and not do anything, be anything, or have anything. It's normal just to sit on your be-nothing, do-nothing, have-nothing stool. That's what's happening in America. You've got complacency eroding America.

Free enterprise means that the more enterprising you are the freer you are. You get progressive degrees of freedom when you've got financial success. Women particularly have got to learn this—the Women's Liberation Movement starts with financial liberation. Once you're financially free, you can do anything you want, you can be anything you want, you can have anything you want, you can think what you want. When you haven't got money coming in the front door, you've got love going out the back door. And every woman, as far as I'm concerned, has the same responsibility that a man does. Figure out how to be independent in all six categories of life that we've just covered. You ought to be mentally independent and physically independent. Consider all those old people who shuffle around and say, "Well, I'm just old and feeble." All they are doing is mentally malpracticing. My father said, "But wait a second, Mark. I'm over seventy. I should get arthritis." I said, "Not if you don't want it." I said, "You want arthritis?" He said, "No." I said, "Then quit thinking about it." And now he's exercising. He's seventy-six years young.

There are four ways to solve a problem. First of all, when you've got a problem, you write it out. You write out a clear, definite, single statement of your problem. Then write out four ways to solve the problem. Pick the best one. Be wild in your solutions and act on the best one. Using this same principle, Robert Schuler started out to build a six-million-dollar cathedral. He wrote down ten ways to get six million dollars. First solution: "Find one guy to give me six million." That one didn't work. Second solution: "Find six guys to give me one million." Costs escalated to fifteen million dollars, and so far, seven individuals have contributed over a million each. Remember: Think big! Third solution: "Find twelve to give me half a million." He found a few. And finally: "Find 10,000 people to give me five hundred dollars for glass windows." And he built his church. The point is that if you keep expanding your options and possibilities, pretty soon you'll solve any problem.

You should also practice a mental problem-solving technique. Sit in a chair and put your feet flat on the floor. Relax and then inhale faith deeply. Hold it. Then exhale fear and doubt. Inhale faith again. Then exhale fear, doubt, indecision, pain, procrastination, guilt, anxiety, and other self-defeating, immobilizing behaviors. Repeat. Then resume normal breathing. This is a yoga practice, and it means that you're put in a calm state of mind. Then close your outer eyes and open your inner eyes. See in your mind's eye a clear, simple statement of the one biggest problem that you've got. Now pick one individual, living or dead, male or female, that could give you the solution to that problem. See that person clearly and ask him or her for a solution to your problem. When it arrives, open your eyes gently and slowly and write it down. If you didn't get a solution the first time, it will come. The subconscious mind never makes a mistake, and there's a guarantee in the subconscious mind. It always magnetizes itself to whatever you ask for. That's why the biblical line is "Seek and you shall find. Ask and you shall receive. Knock and the door shall be opened." Those biblical lines happen to be true. Most people don't ask themselves enough questions, like "How can I sell three cars this week?" or "How can I convince the bank to give me financing?" If you ask the right questions before you go to sleep, the guarantee is you'll wake up in the middle of the night with a solution, or you'll have it when you wake up in the morning. But you must write it down when the ideas come through. Remember, if you ask only for a little, you'll get less. If you ask for a whole lot, you get more. Christ only dealt in surpluses. He took five fishes and fed everybody. *You* too have multimillion-dollar-making talents.

Fifth Commandment

The fifth commandment says, "Ideas are either considered positive or negative." An individual has the greatest power of all—the power to choose to think, act, and/or react positively or negatively to ideas in the form of people, places, situations, problems, opportunities, and/or events. A critical story here is the story of the Chinese farmer who had a bunch of horses. One night the horses got out. All the neighbors came over and said, "How terrible! You lost all your horses!" The farmer said, "Maybe yes, maybe no." Two days later the horses came back and they brought twelve stallions with them. Since things were going well, the neighbors didn't come over. Two days later the farmer's son was out trying to break one of the stallions. The horse threw the boy and broke his leg. All the neighbors came over and said, "How terrible!" The farmer said, "Maybe yes, maybe no. I don't know yet." Two years later the Chinese emperor took all the able-bodied men to war, and the lame son didn't have to go. You see, if you look at happenings over the long term, the reversals, the frustrations, and the short-term problems may be the best things that ever hit you. In the short term, we can't always see how all the frustrations we get are really what's building our characters and strengthening us in extraordinary but very subliminal, very subtle ways.

Sixth Commandment

The sixth commandment says, "Imaginative ideas come in two forms." *Synthetic ideas* are a rearrangement of old ideas, concepts, or plans in a new pattern or form. Ray Kroc, the real instigator of MacDonald's, which sells a billion hamburgers every four months, put together all the old ideas and did it better. *Creative ideas* are received through intuition, inspiration, hunches, thought flashes, and from an infinite intelligence called God. Think about Edison's experiments with the light bulb. The guy kept thinking about it constantly. He used to go into a meditative state in the middle of the day, asking himself, "How can I invent the light bulb?" After such a session, you return to a relaxed, awake state, and you've got a state of consciousness available to you that is tantalizingly relevant and makes you very lucid. Usually, it happens right before you go to sleep at night or right when you wake up in the morning.

Seventh Commandment

The seventh commandment says, "An idea originated, discovered, and invented elsewhere can be improved, modified, adapted, and/or adopted by you." All you've got to do is think of all the inventions that have aggregated. None of us has to invent the wheel, yet all of us can use it and reuse it and use it again. If you think of the evolution of the baseball, suddenly you've got basketball, volleyball, badminton—just improvements, modifications, and adaptations.

Eighth Commandment

The eighth commandment says, "Extraordinary ideas are always accompanied by and followed by a sequence of little ideas that tell you how to accomplish the major idea." Therefore, any idea received, conceived, and believed totally can be achieved. Let me give some short examples. First of all, Walt Disney, after he finished *Fantasia,* nearly went bankrupt. It had cost him nearly six million dollars to synchronize animation and Leopold Stokowski's music. He was walking down the street with his two daughters. They asked him, "Daddy, we've done everything we can think of doing. What do *you* want to do?" Disney said, "Well, it'd be nice if we had a family amusement park that we could take you to." He received an idea. When he started working it out, he discovered it would cost six hundred million dollars to build Disneyland. He said, "I don't know if I can do it, but I'll try." This idea was followed by a sequence of little ideas during the next fifteen years, and now we've got Disneyland and Disney World. Another thinker that demonstrated this principle was Edwin Land. His daughter asked why she couldn't see her photographs as soon as she had taken them, and now we have the Polaroid camera, which gives instant pictures.

Ninth Commandment

The ninth commandment says, "Positive ideas are inspired by a positive mental attitude which is controlled by telling your thinking how to think." Most people say, "I can't control my feelings. My feelings control me." That is not true. Thoughts control your feelings, and your feelings control your emotions, which, I think, are deep-seated in most of us, and our emotions totally and absolutely control our actions. What I'm saying is, decide in favor of yourself. Tell your thinking how to think. Tell your feelings how to feel. And you can literally and absolutely ordain your destiny.

This commandment also says, "Associate mentally, physically, and spiritually with positive, happy, uplifting people." When I was in Rochester recently I visited George Eastman's house. His art gallery had pictures of him with celebrities of his time, including Edison, Carnegie, and Firestone. Everyone is influenced by somebody. Be sure you and your children are influenced by the best.

This commandment continues, "Read the inspired works of great leaders in all fields." Read the biographies and autobiographies of those who have uplifted, contributed to, and helped build mankind.

Tenth Commandment

The tenth commandment says, "The only value of ideas is in their use." You must either use your ideas or lose them. If you work your ideas, they work for you. All of the brilliance of the people we've mentioned in this chapter—Edison, Land, Eastman, Carnegie, Firestone, Disney—would have been lost if they hadn't followed up on their ideas. This last commandment is perhaps the most important. Your ideas are the best there can be—profiting from them is entirely up to you.

SUZY SUTTON

Suzy Sutton was a "Show Biz" veteran even before she launched her present career as a lecturer-entertainer-trainer. She is a veteran in more ways than one, having served three years in the Women's Armed Forces as a cryptographer.

Upon her discharge from the WAF, Suzy resumed her singing and dancing career and appeared in leading night-clubs across the nation.

Even though she started in show business as a song and dance act, her natural zaniness is what gradually led her to the lecture circuit. She has entertained thousands of men and women with her humorous after-dinner talks, custom-created spouse programs, keynote addresses for business and professional groups, seminars, and workshops on the art of public speaking and inter-personal communication.

Her seminar called "Practical Steps to Speaking Up and Out" is a confidence-building, energizing training program to develop innate public speaking skills in any public speaking situation. Another of her popular seminars is called "Television and Radio Tactics and Techniques" and is available for individual coaching as well as in-house training programs customized for each company or organization.

She has had a multi-faceted career. She has produced television documentaries and is host of a weekly half-hour talk show on WIOQ-FM, in Philadelphia, her home town.

Suzy Sutton is a self-starter.

She serves on the Board of Governors of the International Platform Association, is a member of the National Speakers Association and Women in Communication, and is listed in *Who's Who in the East.*

Suzy has appeared on radio and television talk shows in every state. Her enthusiasm and expertise on a variety of subjects from fashion to feminism, from dance to physical fitness, from self-awareness to self-motivation make her a welcome and inspiring personality in any public situation.

She is Ms. Enthusiasm. There are speakers and there are trainers and there are entertainers. Suzy Sutton is all three.

You may contact Suzy by writing to Spotlight Seminars, 253 Shawmont Avenue, Philadelphia, Pennsylvania 19128 or telephoning (215) 487-2920.

SLAYING THE DRAGON

Or Don't Panic, You <u>Can</u> Speak Up and Out in Public!

by SUZY SUTTON

Is this you?

Your boss just chose you, an up-and-coming executive, to present the annual report at the company stockholders' meeting. You find yourself weighing the pros and cons of becoming a carefree beachcomber versus climbing the perilous corporate ladder. No contest! Beachcombing wins hands down!

Or:

You rescued an adorable fluffy ball of a puppy from a swirling whirlpool; the local do-gooders' society wants to present you with an award. Now you must make an acceptance speech just because you fished that scruffy little mutt out of the drink! Why do you have this sudden uncontrollable urge to jump off the bridge into the nearest river?

Or:

You were volunteered to give the opening address at the town's Centennial wingding because you have the loudest voice, and the program site is the park adjacent to the railroad tracks. You're dead certain that you'll open your mouth, and not a sound will come forth!

Or:

You accepted the chair of the "Society to Promote Awareness of the Superior Qualities of Women"; immediately you were challenged to a debate by the head honcho of the "Machismo is the Name of the Game Club." The chair has become a hot seat, and you are frantically seeking a way to get your A-Double-Scribble out of it posthaste!

Myriad opportunities for public speaking confront us frequently. We sometimes fail to see how significant these opportunities are and find it easy to say, "Thanks, but no thanks."

Are you bowing out or copping out? Would you say, "No thanks" to an opportunity to progress in your job, to earn more money, to advance politically, to gain social recognition, to increase your self-esteem and confidence, in a word, to achieve *success?*

The success of both your business and your social life depends to a large extent on your ability to express yourself effectively in a variety of situations. Visibility through public speaking improves the odds of your reaching your goals.

Start today to be better tomorrow. Learn how to activate your voice without deactivating your mind. Learn how not to fall flat on your face even if you do trip over your tongue. Learn how to speak so that people will listen. We all want to be heard, understood, and appreciated. It's gratifying when people are receptive to our ideas in public as well as in personal situations.

So what stops us? In a word, *fear!* The thought of facing a live audience triggers an allergic reaction in most people—they turn yellow! Fear is the ugly dragon that makes us want to throw up, not speak up. The monster answers to many names—stage fright, insecurity, the jitters, nervous tension—making it difficult for us to react in a confident, coherent, and coordinated manner in public situations. It paralyzes us and limits us intellectually, psychologically, and socially, thus affecting every area of our lives.

Obviously, then, the beast must be assaulted head-on with vigor and fortitude using every weapon available. Remember the wisdom of William James, who said, "We do not run away because we are frightened, we are frightened because we run away."

Away from what? If we knew the answer to that, we might not completely stop running, but we would surely slow down to a gentle jog since most fear is fear of the *unknown.*

The solution is beautifully simple! Knowledge will take the steam out of the dragon, understanding will change ugly serpents into a few mild butterflies, preparation will turn consternation into courage, and victory will be yours when you stop the dragon with a magnificently cold stare and scornfully intone, "You can't scare me . . . I *know* you!"

The old timer who sat on the cracker barrel in the village general store spinning yarns and commenting on the events of the day was a natural "public speaker." Few of us, however, fall into that happy category, and all of us need to do our "homework" in order to be successful on the platform. Once you *know* what to expect, and how to cope with the unexpected, you will be able to sell both yourself and your message without selling either one short. Public speaking is a learned art, and anyone who wants to can learn it. Shakespeare tells us, "Things done well and with a care, exempt themselves from fear."

Here, then, are some "Practical Steps to Speaking Up and Out," some super dragon-slaying weapons. These tactics, tips, and techniques will build your confidence and help propel you toward an exciting public and personal life. Who knows, you may find yourself exclaiming, "Today the PTA, tomorrow the world!"

Step 1: Find Out Who's Listening

My small grandson phoned one day and inquired what I was doing. "Pop-Pop and I are just talking," I explained. "Well, who's listening?" he wanted to know.

"Who's listening" must not be an *unknown*. Researching your prospective audience will pay handsome dividends and may avert disaster. Nothing is more devastating than preparing a speech for senior citizens and finding yourself looking out at a sea of teeny-boppers. The opposite is just as demoralizing; teenage jargon will not impress the Golden Age Club. A vivid example of calamity would be a talk on the joys of jogging for an audience of bicycle manufacturers, or "How to Deal with the Stress of Corporate Success" to the American Hobo Association. Why invite certain rejection when a little advance information can make the difference in whether your presentation will show you off or show you up? So learn the composition of your audience. Determine their cultural, educational, and economic background; their ages, sex, and marital status; political and religious leanings; special or common interests; and any other tidbits you can gather. It's a good idea to try and find out who were the previous speakers appearing before this particular group, and how they and their subject were received. Some possible sources of information are: the meeting planner, the program coordinator, the public relations representative, the sponsor, or the conference manager. If you are appearing on television, the assistant producer is the one with all the answers. Step right up and ask; the information won't be volunteered. A little detective work will solve these problems and give you valuable clues that will keep you on the right track while you are writing your presentation. When you and your audience are face to face, or toe to toe, you'll have the advantage of knowing *them* better than they know you.

Consider, also, if you or your firm wants to be associated with this group. Be on the alert for invitations from special interest groups who may wish to exploit you or your company—for instance, the pseudo-patriotic organization which is, in fact, a front for a subversive group. Save yourself the embarrassment of a compromising situation by careful investigation.

Step 2: Find Out Who's Talking

"Who's talking" and "What about" are equally important bits of information. The only thing worse than forgetting what you want to say is hearing someone else say it before you do. Unless you are quick with a quip and the ad lib star of the century, you've got big problems.

Step 3: Think about What You Think

Before attempting to write your speech, or even the outline, *think about what you think.* Now that's not as goofy as it sounds! It is always startling, but not uncommon, to find that we don't know what we think, we aren't sure what we think, what we think we think we don't really, or, at least, not quite! So examine your topic, ask yourself what you think about it, ask yourself what you mean by what you think about it, ask yourself questions about it, answer the questions, then question the answers. Examine all aspects of your topic freely. Don't put fences around your mind; let ideas twist and turn and roll merrily around in your head. Keep the think pot cooking, stir the brew, let it simmer, and the final dish will be appetizing. Plato says, "Thinking is the talking of the soul with itself."

Step 4: Write Something

When you and your soul have finished your conversation, it's time to get organized. Writing a speech by first outlining is the most popular method of construction and the most logical. Outlining will help you get your main ideas clarified and in proper sequence.

The best tip I know is write *something!* Even if you feel your fifth grade teacher would flunk you, put it down. It's much easier to improve and polish something mediocre than to start out being brilliant. Besides, you will probably warm to your task as you go along.

As you write, try thinking of your speech in terms of the warm-up, the shape-up, and the wrap-up.

The warm-up, or opening, is your opportunity to introduce yourself and your topic to your listeners. This is the time to set the scene or the mood and lay the groundwork for your subject. The reason so many speakers start with humor is that it works. It breaks the ice and is an almost guaranteed warmer-upper. A word of caution about levity: If you are not comfortable with it, your audience will be doubly uncomfortable. Take the trouble to learn how to use it effectively or forget it. If you do have the necessary knack to handle it, be sure to memorize all stories and jokes very thoroughly. Forgetting the punch line is like forgetting to close the sea cocks when you launch a ship—you'll drown!

The shape-up is the body of your speech. In getting down to the nitty gritty, lead your listeners logically from point to point, carefully developing your theme by using clear, concise language. Simplicity in structure is essential. Use strong connecting phrases to prevent rambling. Smooth and imaginative transitions will help move your speech to logical conclusions. Help your audience remember your key ideas by using the three *R's*—Relate, Repeat, Recap.

Be sincere; mean what you say. Rhetorical garbage clothed in scholarly eloquence will still be rhetorical garbage and easily recognized as such.

Develop and support your main ideas by the judicious use of statistics, quotations, anecdotes, stories, personal experiences, etc. Don't be afraid to use slang if it supports your theme. Carl Sandberg describes slang as "a language that rolls up its sleeves, spits on its hands and goes to work." Let it work for you.

The wrap-up signals that the end of your presentation is fast approaching. Summarize the key ideas and the supporting data. A powerful recap can be better than the first time around. Humorous one-liners can be nifty exit lines. I find it just as effective to leave them crying as it is to leave them laughing. Just don't leave them up in the air, vaguely aware that you have arrived at the finish line without them.

Your finished speech should excite, not agitate; communicate, not pontificate; persuade, not insist; and be short enough to delight and long enough to satisfy.

Step 5: Rehearse

Having researched your audience, agonized over your topic, prepared your outline, written and rewritten your masterpiece at least a dozen times, it's now time to face the reality that no miracle is going to deliver you from delivering your speech.

What I'm driving at is you might as well give it a go and start rehearsing, always with your tape recorder turned on. Practice alone at first, on your feet and in front of a full-length mirror. Then tackle an audience of one—a spouse, child, grandparent, or the grocery delivery person. Beware of making the plumber or paperhanger a captive audience; the time will be generously reflected in the bill! Bear in mind your ultimate audience will be nothing more than one person plus one person plus one more, etc. Don't become unglued by the comments of your well-intentioned kinfolk; they tend to be the harshest critics you'll ever face. My family's idea of "constructive criticism" is to say, "You're too short!"

Step 6: Learn about the Facilities

As far in advance of your speaking date as possible, contact the program chair person to discuss *your* requirements and *their* facilities. It's a rare but happy circumstance if they are one and the same. Much confusion can be avoided by understanding the terminology. A podium is what you stand *on*; a floor or table lectern is what you stand *behind* and clutch the sides of should you become fainthearted; a music stand is what you might get, as I did not too long ago. A music stand is usually rather delicately balanced on a tripod base and prone to crashing to the floor if caught by an exuberant gesture or a strong draft from the ventilating system. I tripped over the darn thing and came crashing down right along with it! Ask for a nice solid lectern where you can scratch one ankle with the toe of your other foot, and no one will be the wiser!

You may want to inquire if the electronic or print media will be present before, during, or after your program. A camera zooming unexpectedly down on you could make your thoughts zoom off into space. A little advance information, and without batting an eyelash you'll instinctively show the photographer your best side. Get the picture?

Step 7: Dress Carefully

Communication is non-verbal as well as verbal. Since people see you before they hear you, consider carefully your choice of clothes. When selecting your platform attire, don't opt for clothes that will shout louder than you can. Bright prints, plaids, or polka dots may be visually sensational but extremely distracting. The speaker who is dressed provocatively may receive lots of attention but find that no one is *listening*. When your clothes are competing for attention with your message, both may suffer.

Women should avoid wearing glittering, swinging earrings; they can put an audience in an hypnotic trance that even the Amazing Kreskin couldn't break. Likewise, large metal pendants favored by both women and men create havoc when they reflect the spotlight, whether on stage or in a TV studio. Don't think you are clicking just because your jewelry is. Heavy rings thump and clank over the public address system every time your hand touches the lectern, putting noisy exclamation points in inappropriate places. The first time is jolting, the second time annoying, and from then on the audience waits in nervous anticipation for the next inevitable onslaught to their ears and nerves. This makes them a mite testy, and it should surprise no one that it is hard to please a cranky audience. They could eventually become downright hostile, leaving you to wonder why.

Step 8: Conquer Your Body

Fledgling speakers sometimes have a tendency to waken the morning of their debut with a scratchy throat, runny eyes, and drippy nose. Psychosomatic or not, you must somehow cope! Take two aspirin and call your doctor in the morning—*after* your speaking engagement! Chances are by then you'll be cured. Butterscotch candy is good for a dry or tickling throat. If that scotch part gives you ideas, forget it. Scotch will make you neither brave nor healthy. I'm not a teetotaler except before a speaking assignment at which time I wouldn't even sniff the cork of a bottle of rare vintage wine!

Step 9: Schedule Your Day

Timing is a comedic device that gives the ultimate emphasis to the punch line of a joke or story. There is, however, another form of timing, the importance of which cannot be over-emphasized. The problems that may plague you if you don't employ a scheduling strategy will be no laughing matter. Clear the decks the day of your appearance to make sure you have adequate time (but not excess time). Have a battle plan for D day (Delivery Day) that includes the following:

When to Eat: Get some food in your stomach before

the butterflies claim the same territory, preferably two to three hours before you are to speak. Eat before dressing. Gravy-stained ties or coffee-stained skirts are not considered chic. Nor do you want the unexpected hassle of changing outfits. Admit it, we all tend to be a little sloppy at the table sometimes, especially if we are a little uptight. Since dining should be as relaxing as possible, I like to shower first, eat in the almost altogether, then finish dressing.

If you are an after-dinner (or after-luncheon) speaker, I would still recommend eating at home with only light snacking on the dais. Professional speakers rarely get trapped into the creamed chicken in patty shells with *petits pois* routine. They are very adept at pushing the peas around without eating them. This sneaky technique leaves you free to converse with the dignitaries on either side of you who, by the way, are probably battling butterflies trying to cope with the heavy responsibility of entertaining you, the Speaker.

Go easy on the water before you go on and it will go easy on you. A little swig now and then during your speech is OK. That's water I'm talking about! Don't even consider alcohol. You'll not only be bombed, you will bomb.

When to Dress: Of course you have planned exactly what you will be wearing down to the color of your shoelaces or the color of your eye shadow. The trick is to work this into your time schedule so you won't wilt prematurely.

When to Shave: Every man knows whether his five o'clock shadow is on daylight time or standard time and must adjust accordingly. Be sure to add it into your time management calculations. Take an electric razor with you for a quick touch-up if your beard doesn't know when to quit, especially if you are appearing on television.

When to Depart: Early! There's no point arriving before the doors are unlocked, but bear in mind you have things to do when you get there. Plan your departure to allow for the bane of twentieth century living, the unholy traffic jam, and permit enough time to inspect your speaking environment. You will also earn the eternal gratitude of the program coordinator, who's been having nightmares wondering if the speaker will show.

Step 10: Examine the Facilities

Stand behind the lectern for a size check. If your head protrudes above just enough to appear like the sun rising from the horizon, it would behoove you to request or find something to stand on which will elevate you enough to be seen at least from the shoulders up. It is disconcerting to hear a voice and see a face minus a mouth. If you are Jolly Green Giant size, it will be the lectern that needs elevating, not you. You'll feel and look pretty silly if the lectern barely reaches above your kneecaps.

Check the height of the floor microphone if no lectern is provided. No need to strain on tip toe if it's too high or risk a crick in the back if it's too low. Adjust the microphone to you, not you to the mike. Here's an old show biz trick worth repeating: to determine how far your mouth should be from the mike, the vulgar thumbing the nose gesture will do it. Touch your thumb to your nose, spread your fingers, tilt the hand down slightly and let your little pinky contact the microphone. You may have to compensate an inch or so for big hands, little voice or little hands, big voice.

Many speakers prefer a neck (lavalier) microphone because it permits greater freedom of movement. You may have no choice, but in any case test the mike for volume and see that it is operating properly. Don't be shy—*your* voice should be the testing voice.

Lighting also needs to be considered. If you don't want to look like an animated cadaver, don't let them shroud you in a blue haze. Amber light is just as bad, for it can start all sorts of rumors of the poor but brave speaker who carried on in spite of a severe case of yellow jaundice. White spots are fine, but I prefer a soft pink tone. It does wonders for my apparent state of health and is a bit of a temporary wrinkle eraser.

Step 11: Deliver Your Speech

Time's up! You've just been introduced! Great Caesar's Ghost, now what? You slew the dragon, that's what! You are *not* facing the *unknown,* you are prepared, you know what to expect, and this is your shining hour! Advance and be recognized!

Take a deep breath and approach the lectern calmly and unhurriedly. You *are* going to be *good,* so set your audience at ease by letting your smile, your posture, and your attitude tell them everything is under control. A worried audience is a nervous one and one nervous person is enough! Relax and enjoy yourself even if you do have knots in your stomach; treat them just like a knotted shoe lace that needs to be loosened to be untied.

You are at a crossroad, so Stop, Look, and Listen! Don't grab the mike with a death grip and rush into your talk. Instead, stop for a deep (but silent) breath. Greet your audience with a smile. There are lots of them, so look both right and left, up and down and all around. Listen for the hush of expectancy and approval that will signal it is time for you to begin.

Stay loose and you won't collapse. Use your hands, your face and your body to express your individuality, to emphasize and illustrate, to scratch an itchy nose if you must. The key is to gesture naturally. Don't look as though your every movement was choreographed by a computer. Repetitious and meaningless motions are just that—meaningless and repetitious. Waving your arms like an over-excited puppy's tail can be a burlesque unless it is your natural style, in which case it can be effective and entertaining.

Your audience will react *to* you and *with* you. Project enthusiasm and you will feel their interest and response. Give them warmth and they will give it back to you. The confidence they have in you will soar in direct proportion to your own. One of the most rewarding aspects of public speaking is the interaction between you and your audience. It's up to you to set it in motion.

The best tip I can give you is to be yourself. You are one-of-a-kind, custom-made. Nowhere in the world is there an exact duplicate of you, for you are unique! Therein lies your strength. Use your own natural style and project your unique personality. It fits you, goes with the package, so to speak. Imitation is not effective; the genuine article is.

Your general attitude should be friendly, warm, sincere—never sticky or condescending. Old-fashioned stentorian oratory is out; conversation is in. Keep that conversation a little under the time allotted to you. It's common sense to quit while you are ahead.

Step 12: Enjoy

Hear that applause? That's for you! That wasn't so bad, was it? Matter of fact, it was kind of neat, eh? While you are acknowledging the plaudits graciously and with considerable pleasure, you may be so turned on, no one will be able to shut you up or turn you off for the balance of your life!

There is an indescribable exhilaration that comes from holding the attention of an audience, from knowing you have influenced others or at least given them something to think about. Giving is essentially the goal of a speaker whether it is giving inspiration or information, entertaining, or explaining. The more you give, the more you get!

The greatest gift is the one you have just given yourself. You have just opened the door to a richer, more fulfilling life with unlimited potential for personal and professional growth. Margaret Fuller recognized that "human beings are not so constituted that they can live without expansion."

Now you know you *can* speak up in public if you want to. You've learned not to be like the little boy who came home from his first day at school crying and disappointed. When his daddy asked him why he was so unhappy, he said, "Daddy, I can't read, I can't write, and now they won't even let me talk! That's dumb!"

It is dumb! No one can stop you from talking in public or in private except *you*, because you have seen the dragon, challenged the dragon, and slain the dragon that was within you.

Dr. BILL E. THOMAS

Bill Thomas is a man who lives with the principle that "anything is yours for the asking" with a positive mental attitude. Bill has applied this attitude throughout his life to further his education and his business career.

A boyhood interest in magic began his career before an audience, as he learned the value of bringing entertainment to others. He pursued his education while in the U.S. Air Force, studying applied psychology and aviation. Having earned his pilot's wings, he traveled with the Air Force talent show, *Tops in Blue.*

After his military discharge, he applied his positive mental attitude to college, and earned undergraduate degrees in sales and advertising management, applied psychology, and marketing, following them with an MBA and then a PhD in psychology. He also completed the Napoleon Hill Institute "Science of Success" course, which helped him focus on, and encouraged him to share with others, the positive mental attitude that has brought him numerous sales and management awards and records. Bill is also an airline transport pilot and an instructor of advanced pilots.

Bill has traveled extensively in the U.S. and abroad, training salesmen and teaching others about positive mental attitude. He enjoys sharing with others the attitude that has brought him success.

You may contact Bill by writing to 2056 Brookshire Rd., Akron, Ohio 44313, or telephoning (216) 836-8524.

ANYTHING IN LIFE IS YOURS FOR THE ASKING

by Dr. BILL E. THOMAS

I would like to ask you a question. And then from your answer I am going to make what I believe is the most unusual proposition that you have ever heard. Here's the question: If a magic somebody were to appear suddenly before you, hand you a magic wand, and say, "Anything in life is yours for the asking," what would you ask for? Would you be one of those doubting few who would say, "This can't be, magic isn't real, a wand won't work"? Would you be skeptical? Or would you be a procrastinator, one who would hesitate and say, "I don't know, give me some time, let me think about it for a while. Let's see, what would I wish for?" Or would you be one who would speak in generalities and say, "I'd like to be happy. I'd like a lot of money. I'd like a nice position." Or could you, in an instant, describe your heart's desire, what you really want from life?

That's the question. Now the proposition: If you can answer the question, you can have anything you want, because life *is* that magic wand, waving over you daily and saying, "Anything in life is yours for the asking." But you have to know what you want. If you know what you want and if you can put it into three categories, you can have it.

Category one: What you want has to be a positive goal or a positive thing. Or as W. Clement Stone says, "Something that won't violate the laws of God or your fellow man." Category two: What you want has to be something definite, something that you can write down, something that you can be specific about and say, "At this date, at this time, I want it." Category three: What you want has to be emotionally stimulating.

In this chapter, I'm going to address these three categories to prove to you that anything in life can be yours if you apply yourself to a positive, definite, emotionally stimulating goal.

The Positive Goal

James Allen, the dean of American psychologists, said, "You become what you think about all day long." In his book, *As a Man Thinketh*, he gives many examples. A warning is in order, though, because as Emerson says, "Beware of what you want, for you surely will get it." So you must think about positive goals rather than negative ones.

Let's take a moment and explain the difference between positive and negative. Many people say, "If you're a positive thinker, everything great will happen to you." They are wrong, because not everything that happens in your life is positive. But a positive thinker can relate to the most negative thing or situation in the world in a positive manner once he understands it.

Consider this example of a positive versus a negative approach. If I were to ask you to go to the wall in front of you and push it down, what would you say? The normal response is, "No one can push down a wall!" But the first thing a positive thinker would say is, "Okay, I *can*. Now, *how* can I? Maybe I'll need some assistance— a bulldozer, an air hammer, some kind of big machine." If you want to badly enough, you can push down any wall. That's how simple positive thinking is. You can do anything you want to—if you *want* to. You can have anything in life—if you *want* it.

Thinking positively applies to more common situations as well. A group of us would go to our sales manager with plans for a sales campaign we felt wouldn't work. It was too expensive, too time-consuming—we could give him thirty-seven reasons why we knew it wasn't worth the effort. He would sit back and say, "Give me one reason now why or how it *will* work." Think about it. All it takes is one reason why something *will* work, and you can *make* it work. Thirty-seven reasons why it won't, or why you can't, don't help a bit. If you know *why* you can do something, you can do it.

Let's talk for a minute about losers. The guy who thinks he's going to lose usually will. As Vince Lombardi, coach of the Green Bay Packers, used to say, "Show me a good loser, and I'll show you a loser." Everyone wants to be a good loser, but this is a negative concept. Another Lombardi quotation: "Winning isn't everything. It's the only thing." So why should we concentrate on losers? Why should we concentrate on what's wrong with America, our government, our money? How about what's right with it? There is a lot more right with America than there is wrong with it. Negative thinkers, the losers, complain about the inflation of our dollar. It's worth about half as much as it was ten years ago. But let's look at what's right with it. Let's compare it to the Chilean *escrito*. Just five years ago, the *escrito* was worth one dollar. As of December, 1977, it took six thousand four hundred *escritos* to equal one dollar. Who has strong money? Do you want to look at the negatives or do you want to look at the positives?

Here is a story about two little boys, one a positive thinker, an optimist, the other a negative thinker, a pessimist. One day their mother took them to a psychologist and asked, "Could you just balance them a little? What can we do?"

The psychologist thought of a beautiful solution. He suggested, "All right, their birthday is coming up. For the birthday, buy the pessimist a roomful of toys— everything a boy his age could want. Buy footballs, bicycles, games. He's sure to find at least one thing that he likes, and this will start to change his pessimistic attitude."

The mother replied, "Great! What will I do, though, for the optimist?"

The psychologist had an answer. "That's simple. Take a room and fill it full of horse manure. Nothing else, just horse manure. What can he find optimistic about that?"

The mother followed the advice. After the boys were presented with their presents, she went to their rooms to find out if the plan was working. She heard nothing from the little pessimist's room, so she opened the door. There he sat, arms folded, looking around at the toys. He said, "What a bunch of junk. They don't make things like they used to. If I play with them, they'll probably break. If I take them outside, the other kids will probably steal them, and they'll probably rust. Boy, what a bunch of junk."

The mother thought, "Well, that's a useless case. I'll go over and check on the optimist and see how he's doing." From the optimist's room she heard whistling and singing. She opened the door and saw her son digging in the manure and shoveling it into bags, whistling and singing and having a great time. She asked, "What are you doing?"

He replied, "Well, Ma, with all this horse manure in here I figure there's got to be a pony somewhere. And when I find it, I can sell all this manure for fertilizer!"

Positives and negatives constantly affect our lives. How many of you worry about, for example, the 8% unemployment ratio we've heard about recently? This has been in the headlines for several years now. The unemployment is terrible. But how about the 92% employment ratio—the positive side of the problem? It's the highest in the free world today. And if we look at the number of people employed, every year this country has more than any other country in the world. Every year we've had more than we had the year before. This discussion includes our recent "recession." I remember a little rhyme my mother taught me when I was a youngster: "Two men looked out from prison bars. One saw mud, the other stars."

Consider another story. Not long ago a group of meteorologists and scientists accumulated some data and determined that, according to the movements of heavenly bodies and clouds and condensation, it was going to rain for forty days and forty nights, starting in ten days. They said, "What are we going to do? If we tell the newspapers, there's going to be pandemonium, mass riots— what are we going to do?" They decided that the best thing was to tell the theological community, which would certainly know how best to communicate the information to their congregations.

Most of the ministers, however, were negative. They stood in front of their congregations and said, "It's time for judgment day. We'll have to atone for our sins." But there was one positive preacher, who told his listeners, "Ladies and gentlemen, good news. We still have ten days to learn how to live under water." His was a positive approach.

Those accustomed to negative thoughts know that most negative thoughts and goals will be realized. One of the truest stories I can share with you is a personal story, about my own father. He shared a lot of positive thoughts with his son, fortunately, but in one respect he lived with a very negative attitude. He was convinced he was going to die by drowning. He knew this because his grandfather had drowned, his father had drowned, and, as we all know, everything runs in threes. He believed this—he *knew* it was true. So he would never go near the water. I can remember as a young child going swimming, Dad would stand five feet from the water's edge to call me from the pool when he wanted to talk to me or when it was time to go. He would not walk close to the edge of that pool because he knew he was going to be number three, and he wasn't going to take any chances. He always talked about sailing and sailboats, but never in his life did he enjoy the thrill of sailing because he had this definite fear of water.

In our home we had an eight-foot hand-dug well, lined with two-foot tiles. It was in the basement of our farm home, and the little pump on it provided us with water for as long as I can remember. About five years before my father died, we hooked up to city water, and the old well was covered and no longer used. One day, during a dry spell, my father decided to check the water level in the well, just in case city water gave out. Somehow he slipped head first into the well. He couldn't turn to get out, and he drowned in about fifteen inches of water. It's a sad but true story of the power of unconscious negative goals.

You may say that this story was a coincidence, but the newspapers are full of such "coincidences." A headline in the *Akron Beacon Journal* in Akron, Ohio, says, "Fire Destroys Red's Lounge." Red's was a famous local place. The owner was quoted in an interview from the previous summer: "I have a funny feeling from time to time. I love the bar and I feel someday I'll wake up and the bar won't be there, it'll just be gone. You can't realize how bad I'll miss it." Negative thinking? Yes. His mind was thinking negatives while he was being interviewed about success. The negatives happened.

Consider another "coincidence" described in the *Canton Repository* of Navarre, Ohio. The article was entitled "As She Feared, Truck Rips Her Home." A woman had lived in fear for years that a truck would come through her front door because her home was right on a curve. She *knew* it was going to happen. It happened.

An Associated Press article from Brisbane, Australia, was entitled, "Eaten by Fear." A man who had lived all his life in fear of crocodiles was eaten by one fifteen feet long. He was so afraid of crocodiles that he had never waded in water more than a few inches deep. Witnesses believed that this crocodile had stalked the man for days before it attacked and killed him. He *knew* it was going to happen. He'd known all his life. Some people may say that these stories are examples of fatalism. That's true, because we are sharing the negatives. We can, however, do the same thing with the positives.

In psychology, we learn about the phenomenon of selective vigilance—that people tend to perceive those aspects of their environment that are related to gratification of their immediate or long-range needs. That is, if you have something on your mind, you tend to notice the things that may help it or hinder it. For example, a hungry man will notice an apple tree long before a sated person will. If you are planning a trip to Las Vegas, you will suddenly notice all types of articles in the paper about Las Vegas, ads for discount tickets to Las Vegas, people who've gone there, etc. This information about Las Vegas is always available, but you don't notice it unless you're planning a trip. Similarly, when you have a positive goal, your mind discovers many things to aid or support that goal.

Now let's take some positive goals and see what can happen. Newspaper articles support positive goals, also. Consider this headline from the *Akron Beacon Journal:* "He Has a Cure for Self-Pity," about a sixteen-year-old boy from Doylestown, Ohio. When he was two, a riding mower cut off his right foot completely and about half of his left. Even with this disability, he decided to be a sportsman. He played on the high school football, baseball, and tennis teams. That has to take a positive attitude, because the boy who had everything against him still knew he could do it. He shares with us something we should all learn: "When I get depressed I think of something to do. I don't know who told me, but whenever you're depressed it's because you're not doing something. It's like the more you think about it the worse it gets." I believe that is outstanding philosophy and so true.

Another example of a positive-thinking young person lives in Medina, Ohio. This boy was paralyzed on his right side in an accident when he was two. Yet he's on the school track team, and the coach says, "If a kid with average ability had his fortitude, he'd be outstanding. He couldn't help it. This boy never lets up, has never dropped out [of a race], has never finished last, and has made every practice." Now here's a kid who had to learn how to walk by leaning on his left side and swinging his right. He's a track star in his school because he wants to be. This is his goal. What works for him can work for *you*. Anything in life is yours for the asking. Anybody can push down any wall. Anybody can do what they want to if they approach it with a positive attitude.

Norman Vincent Peale tells about a man who went to a psychologist to find out what to do. He had an obsession that there was somebody underneath his bed every night. And he'd toss and turn in the middle of the night and think, "Uh oh, got to get up and look under the bed." He kept looking under the bed and there was never anybody there. He went to a psychologist, who approached the problem with negative suggestions, "You shouldn't do this, you shouldn't think about it," etc. But he had difficulty trying not to think about his problem—his attempts only directed his thoughts *more* toward the problem, which he was unable to solve. He told a friend, "I gave up on the psychologist—he was a negative thinker. Instead, I went to Dr. Norman Vincent Peale. He's a positive thinker. He approached my problem with a positive attitude. He told me what *to* do rather than what *not* to do." The friend asked, "Well, what did he say?" The previously troubled man replied, "Dr. Peale told me to cut the legs off the bed. Now the man can't get under there."

The Definite Goal

If you are going to reach your goal, it must be something definite, something specific, something you can write down in a sentence or two. After you have written down the goal, you should write down what benefits you will derive from obtaining it. This will help motivate you to remember the goal and why you want to achieve it.

Let's take, for example, something as simple as wanting a new car. Many people go through life saying, "Well, I'm going to get a new car someday." And they never do. What they should do is write down the following: "I want a new blue Pontiac, a two-door Ventura, with automatic transmission, stereo radio, and air conditioning. I want this car by January 1st because on the 15th I'm going to visit Aunt Sarah and I want the new car for the trip."

Suddenly, the new car becomes a need rather than a wish. It is a specific, definite goal that you can plan ahead for; you can determine how much money to save each week to make the down payment on January 1.

When you can conceive goals, you can make them happen. Let's take, for example, the story of Pete Gray. Some of you readers who are sports fans may remember him. Pete Gray was from a Pennsylvania coal-mining family. When he was three, a tragic accident tore his body so badly that it never really developed, and he lost his right arm. But despite his handicap, he liked to play baseball, and he found that some people earned money from the game. Now how could he play baseball with one arm?

Pete practiced by throwing stones into the air and by swinging a bat. In time, he developed into a strong one-armed batter. He started playing with a local team, did well, and wrote to Mel Ott of the Miami Marlins asking for a job. Ott answered, "The next time you're in Miami, stop in and see me." Pete hopped the next plane for Miami, eager for the opportunity. He was, however, very disappointed. When Ott saw him, he wouldn't even give him a try out. Negative thinking kept Pete from having a chance in Miami. Then he wrote to Connie Mack of the Philadelphia A's; the same thing happened.

Pete was playing with his local team one time when a scout from the Three Rivers Club in Quebec, Canada, happened to see him. The scout was impressed, and sent him to Three Rivers to try out before another reluctant coach. This coach, though hesitant, let Pete participate in an exhibition game. Pete hit a home run, saved the game, and got a job with the Three Rivers Club. He ended that season with a .381 batting average, to lead the Canadian league. Pete later moved to the Memphis Chicks, a Class A Southern Association ball club, where in one season he had 68 stolen bases, five home runs, and was voted the most valuable player of the league. From there, he went to the major leagues and the St. Louis Browns. He was a man with a positive attitude and a definite goal—he wanted to play baseball in the major leagues. He did it—with only one arm.

Again, I say that anything in life can be yours for the asking. Remember Monty Stratton, who played baseball with one leg. Tom Dempsey kicked a 65-yard field goal with half a foot. And there have been many others who overcame adversity because they had a positive, definite goal. Think for a minute about Milton's blindness, Beethoven's deafness, Roosevelt's polio, Helen Keller's lack of sight and hearing. Think of John Bunyan, who wrote *Pilgrim's Progress* while incarcerated, and Charles Goodyear, who did many of his earlier experiments for vulcanizing rubber while he was in prison. Most of you are not in prison; most have sight, hearing, and arms and legs. We live in a country that gives us opportunity. All we have to do is know specifically what we want, and ask for help or read a book.

It is easy to become a millionaire in today's world. As Napoleon Hill shares with you in his book, *Think and Grow Rich*, anybody can do it in ten years, if you really want it and are willing to get some assistance. First you set a specific goal, then you learn what you must do to obtain that goal. You may be pleasantly surprised when you find out that anything in life can be yours.

The Emotionally Stimulating Goal

In addition to being positive and definite, goals must be emotionally stimulating. Your goal must be exciting, something that turns you on, something that you'll really work for. "Aim high," says W. Clement Stone; "There's magic in thinking big," says David J. Schwartz. People ask, "How high? How big?" Napoleon Hill wrote, "Whatever the mind of man can conceive and believe, the mind of man can achieve."

Consider this story of a man who utilized, momentarily, the almost superhuman powers the human body can muster in an emotionally stimulating situation. Most of us use 10% or less of our abilities; exceptional individuals may use slightly more. This man was present when a large truck and trailer crashed into a telephone pole, crushing the cab with the driver still inside. No one could get him out. The police were called; cutting equipment was on the way. Suddenly, a little trickle of gasoline, possibly a careless cigarette, and the entire cab was engulfed in flames. A tall black man stepped out of the crowd, walked up to the door of the cab, and tore it from its hinges. He rescued the driver. Observers commented that they could hear the metal of the door ripping as the man pulled on it.

The rescuer was later identified as a local dock worker. He was not an unusual physical specimen—just an individual who had been emotionally stimulated to apply his strengths in the proper way. The point of the story is this: We really don't know what potential we have until we're moved by a strong emotional stimulus.

We need something that will really excite us, something that will turn us on. And this is why people with a burning desire to accomplish something, people that really want a specific goal, succeed when others with perhaps more ability and better qualifications do not.

The Power of the Proper Attitude

If we have a positive, specific, emotionally charged goal, we can do anything. I recently reviewed an article in a magazine dealing with nursing homes. Each month, 22,000 people pass away in licensed nursing homes across the nation. However, during one certain four- to six-week period, this number is halved. In 1972, for example, the number of people who died in this period was only 10,800. What period showed this reduction? The month preceding Christmas. The positive, definite, and emotionally stimulating goal was "I want to live till Christmas." If we are sufficiently motivated, we can actually control death. We can delay our death if we have a goal that we want to achieve. During World War II, some persons in concentration camps maintained their health, stamina, and attitude because they had a goal of building an escape tunnel. The odds against them were high, but hope kept them alive when others gave up hope and died.

Hope is that magic ingredient, coupled with a positive goal, that will give you anything in life if you are emotionally stimulated toward its success. I did some counseling in our church, and was always saddened when a mature person would come in, sit down, and say, "I wish I had my life to live over." They were really saying, "I wish I had asked for more. I wish I had known that anything in life could have been mine for the asking."

Jesse B. Rittenhouse probably explained it best in a few short verses:

I bargained with life for a penny
And life would pay no more.
However, I begged at evening
When I counted my scanty store.
For life is a just employer
Who gives you what you ask.
But once you have set the wages,
Then you must bear the task.
I worked for a menial's hire
Only to learn dismayed
That any wage I had asked of life,
Life would have willingly paid.

Take a few moments and write down a positive, definite, and emotionally stimulating goal. Anything in life *is* yours for the asking.

Dr. JAMES J. TUNNEY

Jim Tunney, the man-in-charge, has made himself a success in several careers—education, sports, public speaking, and motivation.

After graduating from Occidental College, Jim began his career in education as an instructor of high-school physical education. At the same time, he began his sports career as an official for high-school championship games. His education career took him from teacher to registrar to principal and finally to superintendent of schools for the Bellflower Unified School District. During this period, he earned a doctorate in education from the University of Southern California.

His sports career is equally impressive. From refereeing high-school games, he progressed to officiating for the

Pacific Coast Conference in both basketball and football, then to serving as referee in three junior Rose Bowl games, and finally to officiating for the National Football League. Since 1960, he has officiated in the National Football League; and since being appointed to the position of referee in 1967, he has been assigned a post-season playoff every year. He has refereed three Super Bowls and is the only official in the history of the NFL to work in consecutive Super Bowls—1977 and 1978.

Now Jim has turned his talents toward his corporation, the Institute for the Study of Motivation and Achievement, and toward public speaking. His purpose: to motivate others to do a better job and to improve their self-worth.

You may contact Jim by writing The Institute for the Study of Motivation and Achievement, P.O. Box 555, Lakewood, CA 90714, or telephoning (213) 860-0555.

"HERE'S TO THE WINNERS"

by Dr. JAMES J. TUNNEY

Dean Cromwell, the late great track coach at the University of Southern California, had an interesting philosophy about success. He felt that, for an athlete to ever become a champion, he had to start thinking like a champion and believing that he could one day achieve that goal. Dean would encourage this attitude by always addressing his athletes as "champ" whenever he met them around campus. He'd say, "Hi, champ, how's it going?" or "See you at practice this afternoon, champ." One day, somebody asked him: "Hey, Dean, why do you call all your athletes champs? I mean, they're not all champions." The coach smiled, and said, "No, but they all *want* to be champions."

Isn't that what we all want in life? Maybe we can't all

be champions, but we all want to be *winners* along the way—in our careers and our personal lives. We want to feel that who we are and what we do is meaningful to us and to other people. In twenty-seven years as an educator, including high school principal and superintendent of schools, I never met a youngster who didn't want to be successful, who didn't want to be *somebody*. I feel that desire is in all of us, all of our lives. We may try to deny this importance in times of stress, self-doubt, and failure, but, deep down, we all want to have an honest belief in ourselves. We all want to succeed at something.

Through the years, first as an educator, and as a National Football League referee, and through our Institute for the Study of Motivation and Achievement, I've enjoyed analyzing winners and those who succeed in life. Champions in sports, business, and other walks of life come and go, but the qualities that brought them success are always basically the same. This chapter will explore some of the personal characteristics that I have identified in successful people, whether they be student body presidents, pro quarterbacks, teachers, salesmen, or business executives.

The underlying trait in all winners is a thing that I call *Personal Power*, as opposed to position power. Personal power has nothing to do with what you say you are, or with what other people say you are, or with the position you might hold. It is *who you are all of the time.* It is the personal qualities you possess. Personal power is crucial, because the more you have, the less vulnerable you are to those people working out of their position power—whether it's a boss at work, a doctor, or a lawyer. Moreover, you can't always rely on the position power you might have to pull you through times of stress; it's what you have inside that will make the real difference. For example, my job as an NFL referee gives me a great deal of position power—as the official in charge of the game. Yet, when I walk out there in front of 80,000 people to work a game (in which both teams want the crucial calls to fall *their* way, I can't simply rely on position power. I can't say, "Hey, I'm the referee—you had better pay attention to me," because that isn't going to work. I have to have a lot of personal power to keep the game under control. You need personal power to keep your own life under control.

What goes into developing personal power?

1. *Self-confidence* is the supreme quality of personal power. It's been my experience that having a high degree of self-respect and self-worth is vital to one's performance. You have to feel good about yourself in order to feel good about what you do. For me, it's important that I believe in myself as a referee, that I have a lot of inner confidence, and that I project this confidence to everybody who's watching me out on the field. I believe in myself, and I expect to do a good job in every game I work. The great O. J. Simpson, for example, is thinking the same thing. He believes in what he does. He runs with the football, and, when he get knocked down, he gets up; when he gets knocked down again, he gets up. He knows that when he doesn't want to get up, he won't run with the football again, and so he's saying, "Hey, I'm a good runner, I can do it—but I've got to get back up." That's the thinking we all have to have. Abraham Maslow has a theory called "self-actualization," but I have my own theory. It's called "self-tacklization." I think that most of the people who fail in life, or fail to achieve their goals, are always "tackling" themselves. They keep knocking themselves down because they've stopped believing in themselves; when they suffer setbacks, they don't have the confidence to say, "Hey, I can

do it—I can get back up." Never stop believing in yourself. Never stay down without a fight. Always think of yourself as a winner.

2. *Integrity* is an important element of self-confidence and self-respect. When I walk onto the football field every Sunday, it's crucial that the people I work in front of—the players, the coaches, and the spectators—all believe that I'm honest and that I'm fair, that I'm going to enforce the rules and do my job without prejudice or vindication. In all relationships, integrity is a key value. You can play it "straight" or you can be devious in a variety of ways. Dr. Ron Brown, at the University of Minnesota, calls it "straight-lining." He says there are two kinds of people: "straight-liners," and "loopers." When you ask a "straight-liner" a question, he says, you get a straight answer. It may not be the answer you want, but it's honest and sincere. If you ask a "looper" a question, he may hold back some of the truth. So if you're going to "loop," make sure you know when you do it, why you do it, and what it's going to "cost"—because it is going to "cost" you. You're never going to get away with it in your relationships with other people. In relationships with yourself, you just won't like yourself as much. Your "gut" will tell you the score.

3. *Self-control.* As an official, I know that I must be in control of myself before I can be in charge of the game. I learned a long time ago that you can't deal with anger by using anger. You've got to deal with it with coolness and an appearance of being unperturbed. Inside, I might be boiling, but I'm not going to let anybody know that he has controlled my behavior. Why should I let somebody else control me? And if they make me mad, they're in control. Not that I don't occasionally show my anger and get mad at a player or a coach during the game, but it's

never because somebody got mad at me. My intent is to be forceful, insistent—and in charge of the situation.

4. *Preparation.* One of the tenets I have in terms of motivation and being successful is preparing yourself for the job at hand. Salesmen, for example, need to do their homework about any new products brought out by their companies, in order to be able to walk into a buyer's office and confidently make the sale. They have to anticipate the questions and know the answers in order to argue persuasively and convince a skeptical buyer. The better prepared you are, the more of your best you can take into a situation, the less worry you'll have. Worry often comes from not being prepared, from not being sure you are capable of handling the job or the situation. I find that, when I know the job that's expected of me (whether it be as a referee or as a public speaker), and I do the best that I can, my level of stress is way down, and my performance is way up.

Let's take the 1978 Super Bowl as an example. Our officiating crew spent many hours together preparing for the game. We were together two days prior to Super Sunday in New Orleans, finalizing intricate coordination of the crew mechanics. We needed to be familiar with the strengths and weaknesses of each official. Of course, at this level, these officials are tops in their positions, so coordination was merely good communication. In addition, we all had been spending many hours of individual preparation—physical and mental—so that we would be ready to perform our best under pressure. One important aspect of our preparation was to get ready for the unexpected. We have to expect the unexpected. We can't worry about it—just be prepared. So, by the time the game began, I felt we were prepared, and we really were not nervous. I expected the crew to be good—and it was!

5. *Accountability.* I've often joked that only lawyers, linebackers, and guys with vasectomies never have to say, "I'm sorry." The rest of us, however, must be accountable for our actions—which is how life should be. I know that one of the greatest influences in improving my own performance over the years is the fact that a camera records every move I make and every signal I give during a game. That film is sent to my boss, Art McNally, and he studies it play by play, every single week of the season. If he sees something wrong, he picks up the phone and says, "Hey, Tunney, I noticed that on the quarterback sweep, you were behind him too far. You can't see from there— you've got to move over a little bit." Now that's great accountability. If you're out of position too many times, they'll get somebody else. In addition, every Saturday afternoon, before our next game, we receive the previous game film for our analysis. The film already has been evaluated, with questions from McNally, such as: "There was pass interference on this play. Why wasn't there a call?" Or, "You called holding on this play, but I can't see any holding on the film." Also, during the game, there's an observer sitting in the stands—an ex-official—who makes a written report on our performance, which also goes to the League office. Our weekly evaluations come from the composite of these reports.

6. *Positive Response to Pressure.* A high performer is generally at his best when the pressure is on. He can really handle himself. People often complain about their "problems." You'll hear them saying, "Oh, I have this big problem," etc. When you're prepared to do the job you want to undertake, you react to the problem in a positive way. If you can look at the problem as an opportunity to use your creative powers, you'll enjoy—to a degree—the effort you make toward solving the problem. With due

apologies to psychologists and psychiatrists, I don't happen to believe that, as a biological species, we were ever "wired" to be "well-adjusted." I think we as a human race are much happier just slightly "out-of-adjustment." When we are too well-adjusted, we become bored and tired with life, and soon we are dead. I believe a person is at his best at moments of solution and resolution. Did you ever notice that you were at your happiest when you just solved a problem? And what did you do then? You went right out to seek a big, new problem. I am absolutely persuaded that man is most magnificent in times of adversity.

7. *Setting Goals.* Goals are important to a success-oriented person; they give him a purpose. We all have to have goals in our lives. A goal is like a magnet to the top performer and the person who's a real achiever. A great coach like Vince Lombardi had a personal strength that made strong men stronger, and one of his greatest attributes was the fact that he had clear-set goals. He knew exactly what he was going to do in taking all those individual players and molding them into a winning team every season. I feel that winners are those with the ability and the willingness to set some goals, and then *to go* after them. If they have some setbacks along the way, they know how to bounce back; but, all the while, they stay focused on their original goals.

Scientists and brain researchers have confirmed that the human brain and nervous system constitute a marvelous goal-striving mechanism that can work *for* us as a success mechanism or *against* us as a failure mechanism, depending upon how we operate it. Present this mechanism with positive or success-oriented goals, and it will tend to operate as a success mechanism. Goals serve as direct means of motivating and reinforcing the self-image. If we don't set goals, we cannot accomplish any-thing significant. Things will happen to us, instead of us making things happen. Our goals have to be realistic, high enough to present a "challenge," yet within our reach. Also, they must be *our* goals, not those imposed upon us by others. They can be long-range or short-range objectives. Once we set our goals, we have to remind ourselves of them constantly. This will automatically create priorities which will enable us to achieve *any* realistic goal.

In football, of course, the *goal* line is an important symbol, and it helped inspire these words by Art Holtz, an NFL line judge and fellow public speaker:

As I pause to think of something that sets
*   some men apart,*
It seems to me that goals in life must be
*   the place to start.*
Imagine playing football, on an unmarked
*   field of green,*
Not a goal line to be sought, not a goal
*   post to be seen.*
It would be an aimless battle,
Were there nothing to be gained,
Without a thing to strive for,
Without a score to be attained.
We must have purpose to our lives,
For the flame that warms the soul
Is an ever-lasting vision.
Every man must have his goal.

8. *Playing to Win!* In sports, the concept of winning is of overriding importance because it's the only criterion we have for measuring anything. If we're going to play the game, then we've got to play to win, because there are only three choices: play to win, play to lose, or play to tie.

The key is to keep everything in perspective. At the end of the game, it's not important that you won—only that you played to win. This same concept can be applied to your working day. At the beginning of each day, when you set out to do your job, you should strive to win—not so that somebody else loses, but that you achieve a specific goal. If you keep failing to meet these goals, if you keep making mistakes along the way, you must realize that failure is part of everybody's success; that you're going to experience failure and mistakes in life. The key is to learn to *overcome* mistakes and learn from them—to retain your self-confidence and a feeling of optimism. Tomorrow is another day. We all fail at times in life, but we must get up the next morning, greet the sun (the sun *always* comes up the next day, and the sun doesn't know whether or not we failed), and give ourselves another opportunity. Don't give in to your mistakes! It's an important realization to fail and to discover that it wasn't the end of the world. You need to be able to see the whole picture—to keep it in perspective.

All of these qualities I've been talking about go into developing a person's character. These qualities permit one not to be intimidated. They are an essential ingredient for living a successful life, professionally and personally. In my own life, for example, it's my responsibility as a football referee never to be intimidated out on the field. No matter how important the game—and I've worked three Super Bowls and a dozen more playoff games—I must have the confidence not to allow any coach or any player or any spectator to intimidate me. Out in front of all those people, many of whom are shouting at me, yelling at me, telling me how bad I am (which generally comes only when their team is losing), it's important that I always believe in myself and that I maintain a high degree of self-esteem. It's important to the game that I give that impression to everybody who's sitting in judgment—from the head coaches to those three "bumble bees" in the television booth on Monday night.

Now to go back to my original theme—*Personal Power*—versus position power. The spectators that I work in front of every week have tremendous position power. They have the power to evaluate me, to reject me, to put me down, and—in the extreme—to try to influence the way I run the game and make my calls, by yelling invectives and throwing things. But these people can only use this position power if I give them permission to do so. A distraction is not a distraction until it distracts, and that's my approach to the crowd: I will not give any player or any coach or any crowd permission to intimidate me. I'm going to do my job the best I can, and, in the end, I hope they like me. But it's going to be tough in some cities. I remember working a game in Pittsburgh shortly before Christmas one year, and they had a half-time show that featured Santa Claus riding around the field in a snowmobile throwing plastic miniature footballs to the crowd. But about three-fourths of the way around, he ran out of footballs—and the people in Pittsburgh *booed* Santa Claus. So, I thought, "What chance does a poor referee have if the people are going to boo an institution like Santa Claus?"

When it comes to facing an intimidating situation in your own life, have a sense of your own personal power, and don't permit yourself to be intimidated by people working out of their position power. In order not to feel intimidated, you need the personal strengths I talked about here. The more personal power you have, the less intimidated you will be. The more self-confidence you have, the better you will stand up for yourself. The more integrity you can take into a situation, the better you will perform—whether it's going into the boss and asking for a raise, or making a sale, or gaining and maintaining the respect of your superiors and your fellow workers.

These are some of the qualities of a "winner." I think Frank Sinatra sums it up best when he sings:

Here's to the winners,
Lift up the glasses;
Here's to the glory still to be.
Here's to the battle,
Whatever it's for,
To ask the best of ourselves
Then give much more.
Here's to the heroes,
Those who move mountains;
Here's to the miracles
They make us see.
Here's to all brothers,
Here's to all people,
Here's to the winners
All of us can be.

Reprinted by permission "WINNERS" by Joe Raposo, published by the Sergeant Music Co., and Jonico Music, Inc. © 1973/1974. All rights reserved.

JOAN JEWETT

Joan Jewett has earned recognition as one of America's top speakers on personal development, business achievement, motivation, and feminity—and she is her own best example of success in all of these areas. As president of Jewett Career School, a private college in Lansing, Michigan, since 1956 she has been proving that women can be successful in their careers and still remain feminine.

When you meet Joan Jewett, who is now a resident of Scottsdale, Arizona, you meet a small woman with an elegance that is at once refreshing and disarming. But when she begins to speak you realize that there is more here than a beautiful woman: there's a hundred pounds of female power that is exciting, informative, and definitely catching. That's why every year hundreds of thousands of men and women across the country profit from her seminars and lectures.

In addition to her being an educator and a public speaker, she is the creator of Joan Jewett Cosmetics. She is an author and has recorded a self-improvement cassette-tape album available through the General Cassette Corporation entitled "How to Create the Ageless Look."

All her life Joan Jewett has been helping others to realize their fullest potential. That she herself has done so—and that she presents her messages with the surety of her experience, with humor, and with delightful honesty—makes her a special inspiration for men and women.

When Joan Jewett says "You Can Do It," you can do it.

You may contact Joan by writing to Post Office Box 4844, Scottsdale, Arizona 85258 or by telephoning (602) 948-5332.

YOU CAN DO IT!

by JOAN JEWETT

Power is something that everybody wants more of. Our desire for power has something to do with a need for security, and it has a lot to do with our sense of happiness. We believe that the more people we can influence and the more situations we can control, the happier we'll be. And since there are always people we can't influence and there are always situations we can't control, we sometimes think we don't have enough power. And that can be very frustrating.

But, though we often forget we have it, we all have the greatest kind of power of all. Each of us has the strongest, the most constructive, the most rewarding, the most powerful brand of power there is: the power over ourselves.

121

Whether you are male or female, you have more power within yourself than you know about, power that you haven't even begun to use. If you learn to use your power wisely, you can accomplish anything. Whatever your mind can conceive, you can achieve. Anything you can imagine, you can make happen. You can become anything or anyone you choose to become. You can do it, if you know how to use your power.

One definition of power is the ability to accomplish something. Someone with power possesses authority or influence over others. Power denotes strength. Channeled properly, your power can do many great things for you and the people you care about. It can give you self-esteem, success in your career, and happiness in your personal life.

This power that we have over ourselves is not the kind of power that wins wars or establishes superiority. It's the kind of power that enables us to be the best we can be at being whatever we want to be. And it comes in two forms, this power: outer-person power and inner-person power.

Outer-person power is our outer beauty. It's the way we look to others, the way we package ourselves, and it reflects the state of our health. You don't have to look like Sophia Loren or Paul Newman to have outer-person power; you only have to take good care of your body, know how to wear clothes, and develop the right grooming habits.

Inner-person power is beauty from within the inner self. It's the way we feel toward others and think about ourselves. It's a state of mind and spirit. It must come from the heart, and we must have an honest desire to be thoughtful, empathetic, and sincere. This power is perhaps our greatest asset, whether we are a man or a woman, and it knows no age limit.

It is the combination of these inner and outer powers that can direct you toward a more meaningful, happier life. When you succeed in applying these powers to yourself, using them to realize your full potential in every facet of your life, then you will become the truly successful person we all can be.

•

A philosopher once said that people are admitted into Heaven not because they have stifled their passions, nor because they don't *have* any passions, but because they have cultivated their *understanding*. Successful people work hard to *understand* themselves and the world they live in. Successful people have a strong sense of self-discipline, and they seem to follow certain guidelines:

1. They set goals

2. They budget their time wisely

3. They consistently maintain an optimistic attitude

4. They take pride in excellence

5. They persevere

Let's talk about goals first. A goal is a dream. It's a personal purpose that you decide for yourself. If you were going to drive across the country in a car, you probably wouldn't start the trip without a good map that told you exactly where you were going and the best roads to take to get there. Success-oriented people know where they want to go in life, when they can reasonably expect to arrive there, and how they're going to go about arriving.

When I graduated from high school, my goal was to attend college and become a home economics teacher. My father, however, announced that educating a girl was a waste of money. He told me just to wait for the man who would marry me and support me for the rest of my life. I did marry, I even bore a son—but after the divorce I realized that, while I was suddenly laden with new responsibilities, I had the power to set and reach new goals. I realized that most women lacked the marketable skills and the self-confidence to get what they wanted from life, and I decided to start my own college for them. I'm now the president of Jewett Career School, and I have been since it opened in 1956.

Remember that a goal is different for everyone. It's personal. It's unique. But it should be meaningful and within your personal capabilities. I think you should also consider whether your goal will help others. Your accomplishments will mean much more if while you have helped yourself you have contributed to the betterment of the world you live in. Of course you can't expect to realize your dreams and glorify humanity in one fabulous stroke. You must set short-term goals that lead up to your ultimate desire. What do you want to be doing in six months? In a year? Two years, five years, ten years—twenty years from now?

One of the easiest ways, I believe, to discipline yourself to reach your goal is to write it out. This will make your goal clearer to yourself, and it will set time limits that will help you to monitor your success. Many people reveal their goals to friends, thinking that the possibility of "losing face" will spur them to work extra hard to accomplish what they've announced they want to do. Also remember that anything you want, if you want it enough, will require that you make some sacrifices. For me—a single woman rearing a child and building a business—the greatest sacrifice was not having enough time with my child and not feeling the love I imagined my married friends enjoyed. Regardless of who you are and of what your goal is, you will have to make many sacrifices along the way. Try to know what they're going to be.

Something else that will help you reach your goal is taking time to dream. Set aside a few minutes every day just for you. Sit quietly, think about your goal, and visualize yourself actually doing whatever it is that you hope to be doing. Use your imagination. You've got to see yourself as you want to be before others will see you that way.

This approach worked for me when I first started the college. At the time, I had just left a $40-a-week job and did not have the wardrobe of the successful career woman I intended to become. And my wardrobe, I knew, was especially important, since I was trying to enroll women in a program to better themselves and prepare for the career of their choice. Although I had a pathetically small budget, I realized that I would have to project the success that I was helping my students to attain. I bought a dress that had been marked down to three dollars and was a few sizes too large for me. To call that dress ostentatious would be a serious understatement of its gaudiness. I took the dress home, rearranged the accessories, and altered it to fit me. It became my uniform. It was appropriate for what I was doing, it fit well, it was made of a fine fabric. Now, if you had used my 1956 financial statement as a measuring stick, there is no way you could have called me successful. But that dress made me *feel* successful, and I was able to project to others the success I felt.

All of us have the opportunity to do whatever we want to do, if we're willing to work hard, change some of our habits, and keep going when we feel like giving up. We also need energy, endurance, intelligence, a sound knowledge of our profession, ability, awareness, an open mind, good judgment, and honesty with ourselves and others. But it all begins with planning our goals. Remember that cross-country drive: If you don't care where you're going, any old road will do. But if you know there's someplace special you want to be, you should know exactly where it is and exactly how you will get there.

•

Each person in the world is given the same 1,440 minutes every day to use as he or she sees best. If you consider all the people you know and analyze the ways they spend their 1,440 minutes, you'll learn a lot of interesting things about what people do with their time. At least some of your friends probably sit back every day, watching the world go by (or *not* watching, which is even less constructive), waiting for something to happen to them. Others spend their days doing things they don't enjoy, blaming employers or family members for their unhappiness, and dreaming about the day when they can do what *they* want to do. And then there are those who have defined their goals and spend their time working toward them.

It isn't the clock-watchers and the day-dreamers who win. It's those who know what to do with their time.

A piece of iron in its original form is worth just about $10. It will double in value if it is made into horseshoes. When it is turned into needles, it will be worth around $400. Fashioning it into fine knives will increase its worth to $2,500. But if that same piece of iron is made into delicate watch springs, it will bring its owner $300,000.

Stated simply, it's not how many hours you put in, it's what you put into those hours. The value of a human being is determined by what he or she does with the time we all have at our disposal. Each of us is our own most important investment—and it's up to us to enrich ourselves by budgeting our time with reason and by filling our days with the learning, the thinking and the working we need to bring ourselves to our goals.

I get up a half-hour early every morning so that I can plan my day and consider that day in terms of my goals. What can I do today that will make me a wiser person that night? Are there parts of that day that are less valuable to me? How can I minimize or eliminate those less-important activities? Of course, there are things we all have to do that are not direct contributions to our goals, but there is something to be learned from everything. Keep your goals in mind always, and you'll enjoy discovering some surprising connections between what you are and what you want to become. Also, the way you respond to unwanted responsibilities tells much about your progress toward success. Imagine that you are the successful person you want to be, and guide yourself through situations the way you think that person would.

I've said that it's very important to take time to plan, but it's just as important to budget that time so that you have enough time left to put your plan into action. Another hazard to good time management is postponement. "Later" can often become "never" when people wait for things to happen to them before starting to reach for their goals. I've watched plenty of women putting everything off until Mr. Right comes along, when Mr. Right was as busy and active and involved as they themselves should have been. So don't postpone your life. Start now to do the things that are important to you.

And while we're talking about time, don't waste any of those 1,440 minutes criticizing or gossiping about other people. Use that valuable time for self-improvement.

•

Unless you want your own personality to prevent you from reaching your goal, you've got to maintain an optimistic attitude at all times. And that's pretty tough to do today with all the negative things we see and hear about. Did you know that for every ten minutes you spend on negative thinking your mind requires an hour and a half to restore itself to a positive state? It's easy to be negative and pessimistic. But all of your fine qualities—your learning, your physical appearance, your good intentions, your openness to making new friends— are wasted unless you have a positive, optimistic attitude.

Attitude is the true reflection of a person. It's also the most basic method of influencing our circumstances. Just as our inner feelings determine our own actions and our own moods, our attitude will determine other people's actions and other people's moods. You know what it's like to be around a person who always expects the worst and has something rotten to say about everything, so you know that your attitude determines how others will feel about you. Just as kindness begets kindness, a positive attitude begets a positive reaction.

As I said, it isn't always easy. But even though you can't always control events, remember that you *can* control your reaction to these events—and you can develop the habit of looking for value in everything. If, for example, someone you work with is getting on your nerves, use that experience to develop self-control. If you find yourself dwelling on a painful experience, ask yourself why that experience was so painful and ask yourself what you've learned from it.

People are as happy as they decide to be. If you want to be happy, *think* happy and *act* happy. If you want to be successful, *act* successful. If you want to be liked, *like*. The way you think about yourself will determine the way you are viewed by others, so that people's responses to us essentially come from ourselves. One of my pet peeves is people who talk only about their problems. They always seem to feel worse when they've finished, and they've usually made me feel bad, too. It doesn't take long before I start avoiding these people, and—look!—they've created another problem for themselves.

If you find yourself feeling negative, change something. Do something different. Go for a walk, take a swim, listen to music you like. You are a very special person. You are unique. That makes you responsible for your life, for your success. And don't fool yourself by thinking that people have good attitudes because they are successful. People are successful because they started out with good attitudes.

•

One of the immediate rewards that you will discover as you refine your power is the pride you should take in your own excellence. Take so much pride in each task you do that you would like to initial each accomplishment the way an artist signs his or her paintings. Perhaps if more Americans took greater pride in what they do—whether that's washing a car, scrubbing a floor, serving a meal, answering the telephone, pampering a client—our dollar value might not be as low as it is today. How can people retain a good self-image if they know their work is less than the best they're capable of? We've all heard that "anything worth doing is worth doing well," but tell yourself that anything you can do you can always do better. *You* set the pace in your home or in your office or with your friends, so do more than what is merely expected of you. Do your job exceedingly well.

When you're proud of your work, you're proud of yourself—and what a boost that is for your attitude. It's also a splendid feeling to know that you are admired for the pride you take in your accomplishments. No matter how large or small the occasion—the way you handled yourself in a difficult situation, the way you worded a letter, the way you ironed a shirt—to know that you are admired by others is a healthy challenge to keep on improving yourself and your work. If you find yourself setting good examples, you'll find yourself working in a climate of achievement.

Young or inexperienced people can profit especially from your desire to have everything done well. Don't ever be afraid to ask them—tactfully, remember—to redo a job if it hasn't been done properly. Always encourage the people who look up to you to take pride in *their* work. Tell them that they don't have to do the very best job in the whole world, but they do have to do the very best job that *they* are capable of.

Take pride in your body. Take time every day to exercise properly, to eat the right foods, to get the right amount of sleep for you. It is much wiser to pay now to maintain your health than it is to pay later to regain your health. Take pride in your appearance—package yourself for success. Advertisers know that packaging is half the battle in promoting a product and it's no less important that you package yourself well. A first impression is usually a lasting impression, so make the *best* impression. Look your best and feel your best. Be sure that your clothes are appropriate to the occasion. Be sure that they fit well, that they're not totally out of style, and that they are of good quality. Be sure that your posture speaks of confidence. If you wear cosmetics, strive for a natural look. If you don't wear cosmetics, wear creams to keep the skin clean and healthy-looking. Be proud of yourself!

And there's no need to wait for you to accomplish something on a magnificent scale before you can start to be proud of yourself. Start taking pride in yourself *now* for the excellence you put into every single thing you do.

●

Perhaps the hardest guideline to follow is to persevere—to keep on keeping on when you fail and think of quitting. It's very easy to want to give up and settle for less. But if you want to be a success, if you want to reach your goal, isn't it worth the extra effort to keep your self-expectations high? Never, never, never give up. Never compromise your optimistic attitude. Never squander your time on worthless activities. And never, never stop working toward your goal.

Many times when I was developing my business I was tempted to give up and ask less of myself. It seemed that there were too many things working against me —my youth, my womanhood, my inexperience, my desire to be a full-time mother and wife—and it seemed that every time I turned around there was something to discourage me from accomplishing my goal. But I remembered that my father once told me: "When you feel like you're being kicked from behind, you know damn well you're out in front." Think about that. If you think that someone or something is trying to bring you down, you must be headed up.

You'll need tons of inner strength to carry on, and it can't come from any other person. It has to come from you. There will be times when you'll feel frustrated and unfit for the challenges you set for yourself, but don't allow those times to distract you from the success you're working towards. Hang in there. Persevere.

We're talking here about self-discipline, and it will help you to keep in mind that discipline is essentially an act of caring. If you give up—if your self-discipline weakens—you are tacitly announcing that you no longer care about yourself. You're saying that you're not worth the success you want. If that's the way you feel about yourself, you can't expect to be respected by anyone else.

It takes plenty of perseverance to be a winner; but

once you're in the habit of never stepping backward and never standing still, you'll find you've got more power to persevere than you thought you did.

•

You are your most important investment. Every investment you make in yourself will pay the dividends of success—business success, artistic success, personal success, whatever your goal is. And personal power is required to make those investments.

You must constantly strive to improve yourself physically, intellectually, emotionally, and spiritually. You must learn to plan and work toward goals. You must use your time with wisdom. You must elevate your personality with a positive, optimistic attitude. Your accomplishments must be worthy of your deepest pride. You must cultivate tenacity, and persevere when others would have quit. And only you can do these things. No one else can do it for you.

But you *can* do it. Your power can make anything you can imagine happen. It can enable you to become the best at whatever you want to be. It can enrich your life with purpose, happiness, and the knowledge that you have accomplished what you set out to do. It can reward you with the feeling that you have realized your full potential, and have therein done something important with the life that you were given.

It's all up to you. And you can *do* it. Says Jewett!

WILLIAM J. McGRANE, C.P.A.E.

William J. McGrane is the director of the McGrane Self-Esteem Institute. He is an internationally recognized self-esteem consultant and public speaker. Bill is a professor at the University of Cincinnati in the College of Business. His most meaningful credential is . . . experience! Bill travels throughout the country conducting one-to five-day seminars for business, government, health care, education, and religious groups. He is a change agent. Bill's ideas work and are used after his programs are completed. His interest, enthusiasm, and timely messages have earned the trust of thousands. Bill is persuasive and believes that, with sound self-esteem, happiness and success are inevitable.

You may contact Bill by writing to the McGrane

Self-Esteem Institute, Formica Building, 120 East Fourth Street, Cincinnati, Ohio 45202 or by telephoning (513) 721-2215.

THE FIRST INGREDIENT: SELF-ESTEEM

by WILLIAM J. McGRANE, C.P.A.E.

*"We need education in the obvious
more than investigation in the obscure."*
—Justice Oliver Wendell Holmes

You are a public speaker until age three, and then you are told to shut up. You start your life as a butterfly, and then may end up in a cocoon. In your first six years of life, you develop a "feel good" or a "feel bad" attitude about yourself. Later in life, you may discover that your attitude hinders your performance in something that is important to you. You decide to change your attitude.

Before you can make a change, however, you have to take the advice of Socrates, who said, "Know thyself." Ask yourself such questions as: Why do you want to better your developed and undeveloped areas? Are you interested in the evolvement of your personal and professional life, of your total person? What makes you most alive? What do you like best about yourself? What do you like least about yourself? What price are you willing to pay for excellence, to become the most you can become as a human being? I suggest that the best way to change your attitude about yourself is to develop sound self-esteem. With sound self-esteem, you can become an outstanding, successful, total person. Only you, by your choice, can develop your self-esteem. Why not begin your journey to self-esteem by reading further?

Evaluating Your Self-Esteem

What is the definition of *self-esteem? Self-esteem* is the way you feel about yourself. It is a warm, "feel good" about yourself as a total person. During your lifetime, you probably have been told over and over again:

"Why do you do those stupid things?"

"You know better than that!"

"You should have been a boy/girl."

"You'll never amount to anything."

"What's the matter with you?"

"Don't you have any pride?"

"You can do better than that."

"How dumb can you get?"

Soon you are controlled by such statements, which make you believe you are not a worthwhile human being.

Because you want personal and professional success, I suggest making a decision to give self-esteem top priority in your life. How do you do this? Stop reading right now, turn to the end of this chapter, and take the Self-Esteem Evaluation prepared by the Barksdale Foundation. To find your own self-esteem index, simply add up all the scores.

Your score will very likely give you a strong desire to investigate the self-esteem process.

The Self-Esteem Evaluation will let you know the level of your self-esteem *at this time in your life*—it is your goal to improve this level. Remember: self-esteem is an emotion, a feeling. It is the degree to which you actually feel warm and loving towards yourself. Thus, it follows that sound self-esteem is genuine love of self. As such, sound self-esteem requires *total unconditional acceptance* (T.U.A.) of yourself. You are a unique and worthy individual, regardless of your mistakes, defeats, and failures, of your human frailties, and of your real or fancied shortcomings; despite what others may think, say, or feel about you or your behavior; regardless of your great accomplishments or lack thereof. Please read this paragraph at least two more times before you continue.

Although the prerequisite of sound self-esteem is total unconditional acceptance, free of all conditional *ifs* and *buts,* of all judgmental *oughts, shoulds,* and *musts,* self-esteem is definitely not egotism. In fact, egotism is a classic symptom of low self-esteem. If you truly accept and love yourself, you will not have a driving need for attention and approval.

As a total person with sound self-esteem, you will not feel vulnerable to the opinions and attitudes of others. You will not be fearful of exposing your real self; you will not have a need to impress others with your worth and importance. Self-esteem is not an arbitrary self-image of what one would like to project to the world. Neither is self-esteem a self-concept based on an intellectual appraisal of your developed and undeveloped areas, of your talents and capabilities. Once again, self-esteem is an *emotion*, a feeling of warmth and love towards yourself; sound self-esteem is genuine love of self. Freeing you of defensive masks and protective barriers is a prime objective of this chapter. With sound self-esteem, you will have no further need for masks and barriers.

The Importance of Awareness

Do you know that it is your current awareness that prevents you from having sound self-esteem? Are you aware, for example, that neither you nor anyone else can possibly make you one bit better, that no one in the entire world is innately one iota more or less worthy, more or less important, than you yourself? Are you aware that you are neither your actions nor your awareness, that you are not bad if you act bad?

Are you aware that you invariably do the best your prevailing awareness permits? Are you aware that if your awareness is faulty it is no reflection on you, that it is simply the result of faulty cultural conditioning by the faulty and destructive concepts, values, beliefs, and assumptions you have been subjected to ever since you were born? Are you aware that the one and only thing you can possibly make better about yourself is your *awareness?*

In this chapter, you are going to learn that the foregoing statements are valid and that you are blameless regardless of what you have done or not done. Once you know this, then you can proceed to develop your personal and professional self, because you will reduce and eliminate all of your fear of failure. Your fundamental problem is that, owing to your faulty cultural conditioning, your present awareness is out of alignment with reality, with what actually *is.* You are going to learn how to get your awareness into alignment with reality based on your own investigation of the observable facts of human behavior, of what you yourself perceive and sense to be true.

What do we mean by *awareness?* Your *awareness* is

the degree of clarity with which you perceive, understand, and evaluate, both consciously and unconsciously,
everything that affects your life.

Accept expanding of your awareness as a personal
passion and challenge. Make a firm commitment to
yourself to expand your awareness in every way possible
and at every opportunity. Make good use of every available fragment of time to develop your personal and professional self. Be constantly aware of everything you think,
say, do, and feel, and search out the motivating need or
cause of each action. Program yourself to be aware of all
your values, concepts, beliefs, and assumptions.

PLEASE STOP. Turn to the end of this chapter and
study the human behavior diagram to see just how your
awareness actually functions. You want to become a
total person. You have your prevailing awareness, which,
as you can see from the diagram, comes from three areas:

1. Your heredity
2. Your inner knowing (intuition)
3. Your total life experience (your environment)

None of these can be changed up to this moment. You
have a bank account of awareness. Your value system is a
part of your prevailing awareness. All of your behavior is
an attempt to satisfy your dominant need to "feel good,"
which expresses itself through desires and needs that you
have on a moment-to-moment basis. When there is interference with the satisfaction of your dominant need, you
experience tension. This tension will cause you to think
about how you can become comfortable, how you can
satisfy your desire or need. For example, you are speaking
to a friend. For some reason, he or she becomes uncomfortable with what you just said. You instantly make a
decision to end the tension; you take action to relax that
individual and make him or her "feel good" again. You

will always know the results of your action by the consequences, which you will receive through his or her feedback. This is very important to remember. You are always responsible for everything you think, say, do, and feel. As you can see from the human behavior diagram, after each action you add to your total life experience and the cycle begins all over again.

The Dangers of Value Judging

What are the damaging effects of low self-esteem? Lack of sound self-esteem is the fundamental reason you do not "feel good" about yourself and about life in general. Lack of sound self-esteem is the root of practically every personal problem. Lack of sound self-esteem destroys your natural confidence and exuberance; it makes you feel guilty, inferior, inadequate, unworthy, and anxious. Lack of sound self-esteem generates anxiety and fear, denies you a sense of inner freedom, self-sufficiency, and competence, of being on top of your life and affairs. Lack of sound self-esteem robs you of inner peace and happiness. Lack of sound self-esteem denies you the love of self, of loving and being loved.

On the other hand, with sound self-esteem:

- You will allow yourself the freedom to accept mistakes, defeats, and failures without feeling unworthy or "less than," without self-condemnation, shame, blame, guilt, or remorse.

- You will be free of a desperate need to prove yourself "better than."

- You will accept your innate authority to do as you yourself see fit and take responsibility for your actions.

- You will be able to release your full potential for

creativity and happiness, to undertake any endeavor without fear of failure or defeat.

- You will enjoy harmonious and loving relationships with your spouse, family, and friends, for you no longer will be judgmental, harsh, and demanding of yourself and others.

- You will enjoy a deep sense of confidence in your personal and professional ability to take on anything or anybody and not worry about the outcome.

- You will be free of anxiety and depression.

- You will experience a tremendous overriding sense of freedom and exhilaration, a joyful eagerness to meet life on its own terms, to share yourself and your ideas with everyone.

What is the major reason that prevents you from achieving sound self-esteem? Without a doubt, it is *value judging* yourself on a conscious or nonconscious level.

What is the definition of *value judging? Value judging* is praising or condemning yourself or others for complying or not complying with your own particular values. Adverse value judgments in particular are identifiable by emotional charging, your tone of voice, countenance, body language, and emotional resistance. They are most easily recognized by an accusative voice and judgmental *oughts, shoulds,* and *musts.*

Adverse value judgments of self are expressed by self-accusation, condemnation, belittling, and put downs, which generate a sense of being "less than," of shame, guilt, remorse, inadequacy, and unworthiness. Adverse value judgments of others are based on the false assumption that they have the same awareness and, therefore, the same concepts, values, needs, and beliefs as you. In other words, value judging is the criticism of yourself or others for violating your own particular set of values. In short, value judging is *finding fault* with yourself or others. Value judgments imply that you "should" have a different awareness. Make a decision to:

1. Stop all adverse value judging of yourself.
2. Stop accepting the adverse value judgments of others.
3. Purge yourself of all condemnation, shame, blame, guilt, and remorse.

You may be fully convinced intellectually that condemnation, shame, guilt, and remorse are not only totally unfounded, but are indeed the basic cause of your self-rejection and "hurting." However, unless you correct your nonconscious conditioning, you will continue to value judge yourself even though you are not aware of it.

Years of adverse value judging, by both yourself and society, have convinced you on a deep nonconscious level that you are "no good." In other words, whether or not you like it, you are programmed with false and destructive concepts of human behavior that make you belittle and dislike yourself, preventing you from becoming a successful, total, fully functioning person. Such negative data has been continually fed into your "computer" and stored in your memory bank until you really do believe that you are "no good," and this faulty assumption is constantly reinforced by both conscious and nonconscious value judging by yourself and others.

If you are to achieve sound self-esteem, you have to work on the nonconscious level so that you will no longer accept adverse value judgments when they occur, and they *will* occur until such time as you have cleaned out your memory bank and turned your thinking around. *In fact, nonconscious value judgments are the single greatest obstacle to achieving sound self-esteem.*

144

But how can you do this after so many years of destructive malpractice? You have to realize first that you cannot stop value judging on a nonconscious level until you correct and replace the false, destructive concepts of human behavior at a deep level of your consciousness. For the law of consciousness, which is just as inexorable as the law of gravity, states: "Whatever you believe and hold to be true at a deep level of your consciousness inevitably manifests itself in your life and affairs."

Affirmations for Sound Self-Esteem

Now since the reality is that you do have false and destructive concepts deeply imbedded in your consciousness, it is up to you to cancel out and replace them with sound self-esteem. You can do this very effectively and in a simple, straightforward manner by repeating affirmations—positive declarations—while you are in a relaxed, open, and receptive state of mind. *There is no other effective means of eliminating nonconscious value judgments, for you are not even aware of making them.* Since most of us have spent a lifetime in planting faulty concepts and values about ourselves, it is going to take some time and effort to uproot and replace them by making positive affirmations about your worth and value.

Here are the basic requirements for effective affirming—*verbalize, visualize, vitalize:*

1. Be convinced of the crucial need for doing your affirmations.

2. Be fully convinced of the validity of the affirmations.

3. Be physically relaxed and maintain your mind in an open and receptive state.

4. Be aware of the full significance of every word and phrase of the affirmation.

5. Imagine and sense the tremendous benefits of your affirmations as if they were already a reality.

6. Incorporate as much imagery and feeling into your affirmations as you can manage.

7. Be consciously aware that you are doing your affirmations because you want to, because they are important to your success as a total, fully alive person.

It is of crucial importance to affirm only what is real, positive, and constructive, only what you truly want to happen in your life. Thus, it is of vital importance to stop affirming such negative conditions as "I can't do that." Such affirmations have a tendency to be self-fulfilling prophecies, preventing you from achieving the degree of success that you want as a total, multidimensional person. *Affirming, positively, on a regular basis is absolutely essential to stop value judging of yourself on the nonconscious level,* to obtain the fantastic benefits available to a person with sound self-esteem.

Thirty Days to Sound Self-Esteem

When you purchased this book, you made an affirmation. By investing your money, you wanted to better your personal and professional growth. You now have an opportunity to make your dreams come true. Here is a thirty-day program which will begin your journey to excellence as a total, fully integrated person. Please read the following eight affirmations aloud three times each day of the thirty days. When you wake up in the morning, stand before a mirror, look into your eyes, and repeat the affirmations out loud. Repeat them once during the day—you may want to record them on a cassette tape. Repeat them again before you go to bed. Here they are:

1. I am free of all value judgments and resistance.

2. I accept myself totally and unconditionally.

3. I never devalue myself through destructive self-criticism.

4. I have unconditional warm regard for all persons at all times.

5. I show that I am 100% alive by thinking, speaking, and acting with great enthusiasm.

6. I am completely self-determined and I allow others the same right.

7. I will write to Bill McGrane at the McGrane Self-Esteem Institute, 590 Formica Building, Cincinnati, Ohio 45202 to share my action plan for making sound self-esteem the top priority of my life.

8. I will send for Bill McGrane's *Law of Consciousness* cassette tape to expand my awareness and reduce value judgments on a nonconscious level.

With sound self-esteem, success and happiness are inevitable. Self-esteem is the first ingredient for your journey to excellence in your personal and professional life.

Bon voyage.

HUMAN BEHAVIOR DIAGRAM

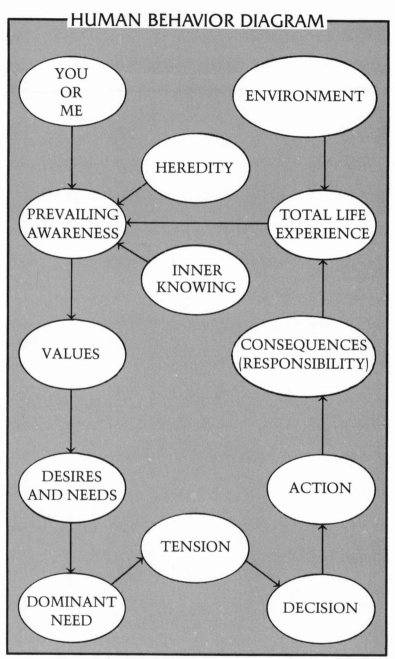

Copyright © 1976 by Liburn S. Barksdale

BARKSDALE
SELF-ESTEEM EVALUATION

Score as follows (each score shows how true *or* the amount of time you believe that statement is true for *you*):

0 = not at all true for me
1 = somewhat true *or* true only part of the time
2 = fairly true *or* true about half the time
3 = mainly true *or* true most of the time
4 = true all the time

___ 1. I don't feel anyone else is better than I am.
___ 2. I am free of shame, blame and guilt.
___ 3. I am a happy, carefree person.
___ 4. I have no need to *prove* I am as good as or better than others.
___ 5. I *do not* have a strong need for people to pay attention to me or like what I do.
___ 6. Losing *does not* upset me or make me feel "less than" others.
___ 7. I feel warm and friendly toward myself.
___ 8. I *do not* feel others are better than I am because they can do things better, have more money, or are more popular.
___ 9. I am at ease with strangers and make friends easily.
___ 10. I speak up for my own ideas, likes and dislikes.
___ 11. I am not hurt by others' opinions or attitudes.
___ 12. I *do not* need praise to feel good about myself.
___ 13. I feel good about others' good luck and winning.

___ 14. I *do not* find fault with my family, friends or others.

___ 15. I *do not* feel I must always please others.

___ 16. I am open and honest and not afraid of letting people see my real self.

___ 17. I am friendly, thoughtful and generous toward others.

___ 18. I do not blame others for *my* problems and mistakes.

___ 19. I enjoy being alone with myself.

___ 20. I accept compliments and gifts without feeling uncomfortable or needing to give something in return.

___ 21. I admit my mistakes and defeats without feeling ashamed or "less than."

___ 22. I feel no need to defend what I think, say or do.

___ 23. I *do not* need others to agree with me or tell me I'm right.

___ 24. I *do not* brag about myself, what I have done, or what my family has or does.

___ 25. I *do not* feel "put down" when criticized by my friends or others.

_____ SELF-ESTEEM INDEX (sum of all scores)

To find your own Self-Esteem Index, simply add all scores. The possible range of your Self-Esteem Index is from 0 to 100. Research shows that an SEI under the mid-90's is a handicap to one's emotional well-being. An SEI of 75 or less indicates a *serious* handicap and an SEI of 50 or less indicates a really crippling lack of self-esteem—one that handicaps you in all areas and that keeps you from "feeling good"—especially from being loved and loving.

What Self-Esteem Is

Self-esteem is an emotion. It is the degree that you feel warm and loving toward yourself. Your self-esteem simply is what it IS, the *automatic* product of everything you were born with plus your total life experience. Thus, low self-esteem is nothing to be ashamed of or embarrassed about. It is important, however, to *you* that you understand each statement clearly and be *completely honest* with *yourself* in order to obtain as true a score as possible. Also, do not confuse your thoughts, concepts and ideals with *how you actually function.* Your Self-Esteem Index (SEI) is important for keeping track of improvement in your self-esteem. No matter how low your self-esteem is, you can improve it as much as you want by working earnestly with the Barksdale Foundation Self-Esteem Program. You may feel better knowing that *everyone* lacks self-esteem to some degree.

Sound self-esteem is as *essential* for your emotional well-being as air is for breathing. If you really want to *"feel good"* on a day-to-day basis, enroll in a "Breakthrough in Awareness" Self-Esteem Workshop. For details, call or write:

McGrane Self-Esteem Institute
590 Formica Bldg.
Cincinnati, Ohio 45202
513/721-2215 office
513/871-4184 home

Copyright © 1974 by Liburn S. Barksdale

NAOMI R. RHODE, R.D.H.

Naomi Rhode is a graduate dental hygienist from the University of Minnesota and has had extensive private practice experience. As a highly successful "people person," she is eminently qualified for leadership in interpersonal communications and motivation.

Naomi is president of Lan Yeppe, Inc., editor of the Semantodontics' Professional Book Club, and a contributor to *NEXUS*, a newsletter for professionals and their staffs. She is past president of the Arizona State Dental Hygienist Association, a member of the Phoenix College Dental Advisory Board, and a member of the National Speakers Association. She has also produced several staff training tapes, including "Effective Telephone Techniques" and "Effective Personality Interactions."

Naomi's husband, Jim, is president of Semantodontics, a Phoenix communication/motivation company with a strong seminar emphasis. Being the mother of three teenagers, two in college, she is especially excited about the challenge of modeling and nurturing successful, happy children. Mark, Beth, and Kathi Rhode are also involved in "people building." They join their parents in giving seminars on self-esteem and goal-setting to children.

A significant part of Naomi's life is her involvement and love for the spiritual part of life, her faith in God, and her dedication to living that life abundantly.

For the multitudes who have heard her, Naomi's warmth, enthusiasm, and communication skills have made her a "remembered experience." Each year she speaks extensively at seminars, association meetings, and conventions, sharing her unique insights in staff training, motivation, and human self-esteem. In addition, she is a clinician and leader at the semi-annual Maui Series Seminars in Hawaii and at Practice Planning Workshops in various locations throughout the U.S. and Canada.

You may contact Naomi by writing to Lan Yeppe, Inc., 5430 East Calle Redonda, Phoenix, Arizona 85018, or by calling (602) 959-5556.

A SPECIAL GIFT

by NAOMI R. RHODE, R.D.H.

There are two words that I think are dynamic words. I think they are dynamic because they can change people's lives. The two words are *inner dialogue. Inner dialogue* is what you tell yourself about you and about the world around you. Inner dialogue can change you, can create in you the impetus for success or the lack of impetus that causes failure.

What's your inner dialogue today? May I suggest a few things? You're probably wondering why you got up so late, and if you had enough coffee, and how long it will take you to read this chapter. You're curious about the subject, "A Special Gift." That might be your inner dialogue.

I think it is important for you to know what my

inner dialogue is as I write this chapter. Knowing my inner dialogue perhaps will help you know what to anticipate. I woke up this morning and I said, "This is the beginning of a brand new day. God has given me this day to do with as I please. It's a gift. I can waste this day, or I can use it for good. But what I do today is extremely important because I have chosen to exchange a whole day of my life for what I do today. When tomorrow comes, leaving in its place something that I have exchanged for it, I want that to be good, not evil. I want it to be success and not failure. I want it to be gain and not loss so I won't regret the price that I paid for the day."

What did you say to yourself when you woke up this morning? What was your inner dialogue? If there were flowers blooming, did you notice them? Did you actually stoop over and smell one? Or would that have taken a little bit too much time because you were in a hurry? Did you hear the birds? Do you know what birds sound like early in the morning? They're magnificent! Did you feel the morning sunshine on your body? If you didn't smell the flowers, hear the birds, and feel the sunshine, it's not because they didn't exist. They were there. They were gifts all ready for you. All you had to do was reach out and receive them. If you passed them by, you missed gifts that were already paid for and wrapped just for you.

What do you think of when you see the word *gift*? A gift is not something that you've earned because then it would be a salary or a wage. In fact, if there are strings attached to a gift, it's not a gift at all. A gift is something you may do with as you please.

There are material gifts. I like them. I like to receive a new watch, a new ring, a new dress. Surely those kinds of gifts have meaning. But I'd like to propose to you that the nonmaterial gifts, the gifts without substance, have a lot more meaning.

When was the last time someone smiled at you with warmth and said, "I care about you"? That's a gift. When was the last time someone was extremely loyal to you? That's a gift. When was the last time someone trusted you? When was the last time someone felt about you in a very special way? Those are gifts. They're nonmaterial gifts, but they're gifts that are extremely special. I'd like to share with you my experience with that kind of gift.

I was raised in the Midwest, in Fargo, North Dakota. My midwestern home taught me a kind of gift-giving philosophy. Think back to the gift-giving philosophy of your past. Was it the kind of philosophy where a five-dollar gift was given for whatever happened in your life? Maybe a five-dollar gift was given when you were born, and you received a five-dollar gift for your birthday and for Christmas. And when a person died, he usually was given a five-dollar memorial. Of course, he got the memorial after everyone checked in the book and found out that his other friends and relatives also gave five dollars. I remember as a child wondering about that. Was that really what it was all about? A keeping-score philosophy?

There's a verse that I love in a paraphrased version of the New Testament. It says: "The measure you use to measure with is the very same measure that's used to give back to you." That is, the container you use to give your gift is the same container that's used to give a gift back to you. What size container do you use? A thimble? A coffee can? A wash tub?

In this fantastic home where I was raised in Fargo, North Dakota, I had parents who modeled an unusual philosophy of gift-giving, unlike the keeping-score philosophy of the society around us. I remember one Christmas Eve. It was snowy and it was very cold. We were going to open our gifts around the Christmas tree after eating our traditional oyster stew. We sat down and my dad said, "Before we open our gifts, we're all going to pile into the Plymouth and go for a ride." Now that was a gift in itself in 1946. Gas was rationed, and it was really a gift to go for a ride. We hopped into the car and started down to the Skid Row section of town. My dad said, "We're going to find someone who is a stranger, who's cold, who's lonely, and who's sober. We're going to invite him to come and spend Christmas at our home." And we did. We found someone who was cold, lonely, and sober to come and share Christmas with us. My father's action was a model of gift-giving. The lonely man became our friend. He was an itinerant farm worker who was left over from harvest and was waiting for springtime planting.

Has your inner dialogue allowed you to serve as a good model for your children, as my father did? My father was a great philosopher in his own right. He taught us a philosophy of living by his actions and by telling stories. I'll never forget one of the stories because it relates to gift-giving.

My father told me about a little shopkeeper back in the Depression days. He said people acted very strangely during the Depression. They started to hoard—everything they could get they hung onto. This shopkeeper was unique because he had the finest scales for weighing that were available. No cheating. When you came into his store to purchase some flour, sugar, or coffee beans, the storekeeper carefully scooped the merchandise from the barrel into the shiny scales. He'd scoop until the side with your purchase exactly balanced the five-pound weight on the other side. Then he would take one more scoop and make a nice rounded heap; the scale would go down in favor of you, the customer. The shopkeeper would look you square in the eye with a warm kind of eye contact and he'd say, "Lan yeppe." *Lan yeppe* means "every bit you paid for and then just a little bit more, which is worth all the rest in life."

My dad was a very profound man. When he told me this story, he added, "Naomi, do you know how to be successful in life? All you have to do is to be *lan yeppe*. All you have to do is give every bit you're paid for and then just a little bit extra. That's the gift. Just a little bit extra, which is worth all the rest in life. Be a *lan yeppe* friend. Be a *lan yeppe* wife. Be a *lan yeppe* mother. Be a *lan yeppe* worker. Then you'll find success in life." His inner dialogue was very wise.

The world turns, and all of a sudden I'm a parent. I wonder if my inner dialogue allows me to be a good model for my children. What kind of gifts am I giving to my children? My husband and I have three of the neatest teenage children in the whole world. Sometimes they surprise me and come to hear me speak. That's a gift. But what do I give to them? I give my whole self. Do you? Now all we parents give ourselves genetically, whether we like it or not. We give ourselves environmentally. We give ourselves as a model, good or bad. I give *lan yeppe* support to my children. I give trust to my children. Do you know what they say to me? "Mom, do you know that our friends' parents don't trust them? Why is that?" Do you give this gift of trust to your teenage children? I believe it makes all the difference in the world. I give love to my children. My children give back love and an open responsiveness that humbles me right to my knees some days in thanksgiving. They support me as a person—they give *lan yeppe* support, and respect.

What gifts do you give to your friends? Who are your friends? If I asked you to write down a list of the significant others in your life, who would they be? Do you know? I hope so, because I ask you to pour yourself into your friends. What gifts do you give to your friends? Do you give your friends openness? Do you drop those heavy masks? We all wear masks to church, to lunch, to meetings. Do you drop them for your friends? Can you say, "It's good to be with you. It's good to kick off my shoes and just be with a friend"? Do you give trust to your friends? Do you give time? Only when it's convenient? Or are you the kind of friend who always says, "Sure, I have time to listen"? Do you give the gifts of time and attention to your friends?

What gifts do you give to your business associates? Do you give them the "gift" of unrestrained jealousy? Do you try to find some error in what they're doing? Or do you give them support? Do you share ideas with them? If you're the kind of person who gives openness, you'll have so many ideas that no one could keep up with you anyway, even if they tried. Do you give your business associates the gifts of openness and sharing?

My husband and I are in a very exciting business. We give seminars for physicians, dentists, and their staffs. We speak to these professional groups all over the United States, and we're very careful to pick the nicest places to give seminars. We often choose Hawaii. We go there twice a year, in July and January, to give these seminars.

An exciting thing that relates to gift-giving happened to me in Hawaii last January. I had been asked before I left for Hawaii to give a Valentine's Day speech at a large couples club banquet in a California city when I came back from Hawaii. The organization had stacked the deck a little bit in advance. They said, "Now we want you to know that last year's speaker was Pat Boone, and the speaker before that was Mark Hatfield, and we've never had a woman speaker. We don't want you to be nervous or anything, but the audience doesn't know who Naomi Rhode is, they've never heard of Naomi Rhode. They're asking 'Who is Naomi Rhode?' and you're going to speak on *what*? On gift-giving?" Well, I don't know what you do when the deck is stacked against you, but I ask for help because I've got a source of help, up above. So I asked my source, "Ok, in Hawaii I need a *message* on gift-giving. Would you give it to me?" And He did! He does do those kinds of things, you know, for me, and for you if you ask.

We went to Hawaii. One of our goals during seminars is to get to know the participating couples as well as we can. We usually try to have our meals with individual couples. One morning we went to breakfast with a young dentist and his wife, Dave and Carol. We had a delightful breakfast; it was really the first time we'd spoken to them personally and privately. As Carol and I walked to the seminar meeting room, she said, "I'm going to be a little late. I just have to step into this dress shop for a minute." We gals do that occasionally. When she came into the seminar, I asked, "Did you find something to buy?" I thought maybe I could find something if she had. She replied, "Oh, Naomi, I saw the most beautiful dress! It's long and it has quilting around the sleeves and quilting around the bottom. It's just beautiful but I didn't buy it. I just musn't right now."

We sat down at the seminar in a big circle and started our dialogue laughing and talking. All of a sudden I got it! I got the message I had asked for in the form of a directive: "Why don't *you* go and buy that dress for Carol?" Now that was a very strange directive, one I'd never had before. I often have directives to buy myself a dress, but I never particularly had one to buy someone else a dress. So I thought, "I'll check it out with my husband. Certainly he will put a kibosh on this quickly." So I went to him and said, "I feel like I should go buy Carol a new dress." He replied, "Go and do it. Go right now." *That's* a gift. Do you support your spouse like that? I walked out of the room, feeling trembly, wondering, "What am I doing? I'm walking to the dress shop not knowing what size she is, not knowing which dress it is, not knowing how much it costs."

I walked into the dress shop and there, in the middle of the room, on a mannequin, was this beautiful long dress with quilting on the sleeves and quilting around the bottom. I asked the sales clerk, "Was there a cute blond gal in here looking at that dress?" She said, "Yes, she's been in here several times, as a matter of fact." I said, "Oh, great, then I want to buy that dress for her as a gift."

It was as if that saleswoman sprouted horns. She looked at me and said, "Oh, you're buying it for her—you must be *very* good friends."

I said, "Well, not really."

This saleswoman had the gift-giving philosophy we all often have. "Why, then," she said, "it must be her birthday."

"No," I replied, "I don't think it's her birthday."

"Well, then she must have done you a favor."

"No, not really."

"Then why do you want to buy her a gift?"

"Just because I *want* to buy her a gift. A surprise box. Would you wrap it up and put beautiful paper on it and a big bow?"

The saleswoman seemed almost reluctant to do so. By the way, I had not looked at the price. I just decided it wouldn't be fair to myself. I took the gift to the hotel front desk and asked for Carol's room number. They gave it to me. I went up to the floor, the maid opened the room, and I left the box on the bed, without a card or note, and went back to the seminar.

During the seminar, I started to watch what was happening, especially on Carol's face. She was having a delightful time. She was talking, laughing, and enjoying the seminar. I felt almost deflated for a moment because I realized she didn't *need* the dress. She was perfectly happy without it. But then I realized the message of gift-giving that I had asked for was here. The message said, "Do you know that *all* the beautiful and exciting boxes and gifts in life are *already purchased for you?* They are purchased, they are wrapped, they have bows on them, just like Carol's dress. They are beautiful gifts of self-actualization that are yours but for the receiving. The giving isn't all there is to a gift. The receiving is absolutely as important as the giving."

I knew that Carol couldn't check out of the hotel without returning to her room. She had to go back to the room or she would be unable to receive that beautiful surprise that was all ready for her. All of a sudden it was as if someone were saying to me, "Hey, do you know all the neat things that are prepared for *you?* Have you *any* idea of all the surprises that are already paid for and waiting for you, Naomi? But you've got to follow the right path, as Carol has to go back to the room. You've got to grow. You've got to care. You've got to share. You've got to love, laugh, and follow the direction that I've planned for you. And you're going to find those gifts."

Well, I was so excited about what I had been told about gift-giving that I almost forgot that Carol had been given the dress. I had already gotten my return on that gift.

My husband and I were back in our room, just sitting and visiting and enjoying Hawaii, when there was a knock on the door. Dave and Carol came in looking rather pale and strained. Carol said to me, "Naomi, do you know anything about that dress in my room?"

I smiled and said, "What dress?"

She started to cry, "Oh, I didn't expect that!"

Then I looked at Dave, and he also had tears in his eyes.

Carol continued, "Naomi, I don't understand. Why did you love me enough to give me a gift when you didn't even know me? No one has ever loved me that much."

I said, "Well, if you sit down a minute, I'll tell you why I gave it. You know, you're going to think this is strange, but I really felt that I was *asked* to give it to you. And do you know what I have learned as a result? Carol, do you know that, if you hadn't gone back to your room, you would have missed the box? I have learned that there are unlimited surprises in store for Naomi, throughout my entire life, if I follow the *right path,* as you did when you went back to your room. I am so excited about what I've been taught that now, if you enjoy the gift, you give me a special bonus." We talked a bit more, and they left.

The next morning they joined us again for breakfast. Carol said, "Now I want to tell you what you really gave to me. You don't even know yet." It is interesting how many meanings gifts can have. Carol went on, "You know, I was born an identical twin. I was born first, so I was considered the strong one. I went through grammar school and high school as the strong one. I was the one who held things together. Then I married Dave. He's sensitive and warm and I've been the more controlled one emotionally in our marriage. A few years ago I realized I had never given myself the privilege of tears. I have never in my adult life cried in front of another person. I wanted to badly, but I couldn't because I was the strong one. Then when I walked into your room and realized your love when you hadn't even known me, I realized that I had gotten the gift of tears. I cried for the first time in my life as an adult. And of course Dave had never seen me cry. His tears were because of mine. Thank you for the gift of tears."

Then I had to ask, "What did you feel about the spiritual message that *I* received?"

She said, "That was fascinating. You know, we don't have a spiritual faith, but we've been interested in looking for one. We'd really like to research yours."

They did. They accepted that faith. Spiritual faith is a gift, you know. It's not something we work for. It's a gift.

I recommend that you read a little book by Paul Turnier, a Swiss psychiatrist, entitled *The Meaning of Gifts.* It heightened my awareness of gift-giving, and it can cause you to think more about gift-giving. What is a gift? A dress, perhaps. Tears, perhaps. Spiritual faith, perhaps.

There is another verse of scripture that I really want to share with you because I think it's so special. It is found in a paraphrased version of the Proverbs. It goes like this: "Do you know that it's possible to give away and become richer? It's possible to hold on too tightly and lose everything." Maybe that's what you're doing with your teenagers—holding on so tightly that you're going to lose them. "Yes," the verse continues, "the liberal man shall be rich. By watering others, he waters himself." Are you that kind of gift-giver?

What gifts do you give to your spouse? To the person you chose to live with, to spend your life with? It was your choice, you know. What gifts do you give to the person you're in love with? Are you in love with anyone? Do you know how wonderful love is as a gift? What kinds of gifts do you give to each other in your marriage? Do you give your whole self and in return receive back a much fuller, more beautiful self?

There's a little phrase that my husband and I have heard that we love. I'd like to give it to you. Perhaps you'd like to tack it up on your mirror or, at least, in your heart, because I believe it affects marriages significantly. I believe it's a gift. It goes like this: "Be gentle." There's a gift to being gentle. "Be kind." There's a gift to that. "Be honest with yourself." That's a very important gift you can give to yourself. "And, above all, love one another." Put together, it says: "Be gentle, be kind, be honest with yourself, and, above all, love one another."

What gifts do you give to your spouse? May I propose to you that your marriage is not a private affair? It affects me. My marriage affects you. It's a gift I can give to you as my friend, and it certainly affects our children.

Christ said when he was here on earth that we are to love one another as he loved us. What an example! He was willing to give his whole life even for his enemies. We are to love one another as he has loved us.

I know you want to do something with what you are learning in this chapter. Now this is just for those readers who would like to grow *today*. The rest can forget it, and stop reading here.

Right now, in your inner dialogue pick one person that you love. If you don't love even one, you're in trouble. Maybe it's a husband, a wife, a child, a friend, or a colleague. Today, write that person a "love letter." It may be the nicest gift that your person has ever received. I've gotten some of those gifts, and I cherish them. And it might do something for *your* soul, too. Consider this poem:

What is that that you hold in your hand?
Oh, nothing, you say, but look again.
Every hand holds some very special gift.
A hammer, maybe, a broom.
A pen, a hoe, or a scalpel.
An artist's brush, a needle,
A microscope, a violin's bow.
Maybe a way with words
In the giving of faith and hope.
What is that that you hold in your hand?

Whatever the gift may be,
It can open the door to abundant life.
You hold in your hand the key.

When I speak to a group, I give them gifts. I may give material gifts to the person who introduces me, to the people who help me. They have given me gifts, which I have received. My gifts to them are theirs only if they come to receive them. Otherwise, they are still mine. Then I give all listeners, as I am going to give all my readers, verbal gifts. I want you to know that I have enough for everyone who listens to me speak and for every reader of this chapter. I have a bag full, and I don't have to be present to hand them to you. The exciting thing, though, is they're yours *only* if you'll say, "Yes, I'll take that one!" You need to reach out and receive my verbal gifts within your heart and soul if they are to be yours.

The first gift I'd like to give you is health in this next year, health like you've never experienced before. You know what that means? Running, jogging, playing lots of tennis.

Then I'd like to give you the gift of being emotionally healthy, like you've never been before. You must "put it together," and know that you can laugh, cry, shout, praise, and live the abundant life emotionally.

Next is the gift of intellectual health. Do you know that there is not a single reader who has achieved more than 4 to 6% of his or her potential? Can you imagine what will happen to you if you self-actualize and grow just 1% more this year? I'd like to give you that gift, if you'll reach out and take it.

I'd like to give you the gift of spiritual health because you're a spiritual person. And unless you find faith in God, I don't believe you're developed to your highest personal potential. But that, too, is a gift you'll have to reach out and receive.

Another gift is the gift of knowing who you are in a way that you've never known this year. That's important because the message is no greater than the messenger, and all people are messengers. That is, your message will be no greater than you are as a person. Find out who you are this year in a way you've never known before. And then I'd like to give you the gift of learning how to share this message. That's what you're here for. You've got a message. How do you share it with other people? I'd like to give you the gift of finding the way to share your message in a dynamic way.

I'd like to give you the gift of enjoying a family relationship like I have, of giving gifts and receiving them from children and from your spouse. I'd like to give you the gift of having a love relationship in your marriage like I have—a supportive, wonderful relationship. But you've got to reach out and receive that gift.

And finally, I want to give you the gift of laughing and loving and praying and climbing mountains and singing songs, and doing all those wonderful things that are yours to do.

In closing, I'd like to thank you for some gifts. You've given them, you know. I'd like to thank you, first, for the gift of invitation. By reading this chapter, you've invited me to speak to you. That is a phenomenal gift—to be invited to share me with you. And I thank you for the gift of celebration. Do you know that "every meeting of persons is a unique exchange of gifts"? Any time we're together as persons, as speaker and listener or as writer and reader, it's a celebration. Thank you for celebrating life with me.

WILLIAM G. FITZ-HUGH

When you want the "Voice of Experience" to address your group, call Bill Fitz-Hugh. Bill is a seasoned business executive who, through his selling and motivational skills, built the annual sales of Smith's Transfer Corporation of Staunton, Virginia, from $2 million to $125 million by the time he retired. He added almost $5 million in new sales volume for every one of his twenty-eight years with that company.

In the process, Bill Fitz-Hugh built and motivated an organization of 200 sales professionals and became a senior vice president and member of the board of directors.

Today, Bill Fitz-Hugh is retired; but his retirement is in name only. Now, he travels the length and breadth of this land sharing his inspiring, motivational thoughts at meetings and conventions of boards of realtors, insurance groups, trade associations, corporations large and small, sales groups, and financial executives. He delights in sharing his ideas from time to time with young people on university campuses. Regardless of where you find Bill Fitz-Hugh speaking, you will find an audience both moved and inspired by his warm and professionally seasoned manner. This chapter is but a sample of Bill Fitz-Hugh's common sense.

You may contact Bill by writing to 23 Woodland Drive, Staunton, Virginia 24401, or telephoning (703) 886-7427.

THE VALUE OF YOUR NAME

by WILLIAM G. FITZ-HUGH

Before any of us ever started kindergarten, we instinctively felt the urge to fight if anyone made fun of our name. Even at that early age, we assigned a value to our name.

Later, as we matured into adults, we came to feel the need to be of value as a person, not only to ourselves, but also to others. As adults, we give new and different dimensions to the value of our name. There are at least four dimensions of value. First there is the value we ourselves place on our name—some call this self-esteem. Second is the value others place on our name—this is the way others see us, the way we appear to others. Third is the way we *want* others to see us—that is, we want others to respect us and to be aware of our integrity. And finally, there is the true value of our name—an objective, fair appraisal of our innermost character and worth. This

173

chapter gives a number of examples and stories that help us understand and evaluate these different values of our name.

The Value of Our Name
— A Need for Commitment

As recently as a hundred years ago, merchants did not display price tags on their goods. When a customer found an item he wanted, he would ask the price. Often, the customer would argue and complain about the price, pointing out the laws of supply and demand. In defense, the merchant would attempt to demonstrate the quality of the product. He would also point out the large investment in the range of goods he was able to offer the customer.

Visualize a woman purchasing cloth. As she examined the merchant's goods, feeling the cloth for quality and texture, she would haggle over the price. After an agreement had been reached—and only then—would the merchant take the bolts of material over to the measuring counter and actually cut the material. The various markers on the measuring table were made of brass— brass tacks. Only when the merchant and his customer "got down to brass tacks" was the irreversible step of cutting the cloth taken.

As the merchant waited to cut the cloth until his customer had committed to paying a certain price, we have to be committed to building a certain value into our name before we can cut the cloth of success. We have to be willing to "get down to brass tacks" with ourselves, or we will never obtain the full measure of success of which we are capable.

The Importance of Careful Goal-Building

Now and then, as we struggle to build the value of our name, we sometimes get side-tracked. We settle for less than full measure. We pursue goals that are not all they appear to be on the surface. Let me illustrate.

When I was a boy, the arrival of the circus in town was the highlight of the whole summer. If you are old enough, you may remember seeing the advance team come through town three to four weeks before the circus itself was scheduled to arrive. They placed very colorful signs on every telephone pole, every power pole, and even some of the highway signs. Usually, the store owners would permit the circus people to place their signs in shop windows.

On one occasion, I'm told, a young boy living in a small midwestern town saw these signs. He had always wanted to see the circus but had never been able to afford the admission price. This year, he decided, was going to be different; he was going to save his money and see the circus.

After waiting for what seemed like forever, the glorious day finally arrived. The boy got up early and stood on a street corner waiting to see the circus come by. At the railroad station, the circus train began to discharge the wagons loaded with animals and all the paraphernalia it takes to make the circus the spectacle that it is. After the train was unloaded, the wagons began to move out toward the circus grounds. The parade passed by the boy standing on the street corner.

First came the elephants. In the lead was the largest of these giant animals with a beautiful lady balanced on its head. Next came the wagons, pulled by teams of horses. Of course, many of the wagons were loaded with animals in cages. And bringing up the rear of this huge parade was the circus band, playing music the boy had never heard before.

The very last instrument was a huge bass drum. One man carried it strapped to his back while another followed closely behind, pounding it on both sides and making an almost deafening Boom! Boom! Boom!

After all the other parts of the parade had passed, the boy walked up to the man carrying the bass drum, handed him his money, and went home—thinking he had seen the circus. He didn't even know there was a big top. Because he hadn't learned what the circus really was, three years passed before he found out that he had missed the real thing. So if you are making a commitment to developing the value of your name and reaching success, you must understand exactly what you want to attain. Then you must motivate yourself to attain it. But all the motivation in the world—like the young boy who saved his money for the circus—won't help if you don't understand where you're going.

What Your Name Means to You
— The Value of Self-Esteem

People who place a low value on their name and have low self-esteem often have difficulty with goals and with motivation. Consider this story.

Some time ago, I spent a very relaxed afternoon with a friend of mine. We had enjoyed a late lunch and then sat around drinking coffee, bringing each other up to date on family activities and home occurrences. During the course of the visit, he asked how I was enjoying my retirement. "Just fine," I told him, "as long as I stay busy preparing to give a talk or seminar or writing an article."

"But I thought you retired so you wouldn't have to work," he said.

"You're right," I acknowledged, "but I don't consider sharing my experiences with you or with others as work. Rather, it's something I need to do if for no reason other than my own peace of mind. I feel a sense of purpose in attempting to be of help to others who want to improve their lives."

After pondering a moment, my friend said, "You know, Bill, I've been unemployed for a long time. It's been at least six months since I even made a serious attempt to get another job. Will you do something to motivate me so I can get out and start looking for a job again?"

"I'm sorry," I told him, "but I couldn't do that even if I wanted to. Motivation is an *inside* job. I can give you some ideas you can use to motivate yourself if you have a sincere desire. But before I do, tell me what happened to that last job lead I gave you? At your request, I called a large company nearby and asked about their need for a person with your education and management experience. Whatever happened to that lead?"

Sheepishly, he said, "I don't know. I didn't follow it up. In fact, I've had other friends make inquiries for me at companies in the area. They've turned the information over to me to check out, but I just haven't done anything with it. Now that you ask, I'm sorry I even brought up the subject, because now you know I've been wasting your time. You and the others have tried to help me, but I didn't even make a phone call or write a letter. Bill, can't you tell me anything to get me moving again? I just can't seem to get off my duff and look for a job."

"No, I cannot," I answered. "I truly wish I could, but I firmly believe that we all do exactly what we want to do."

"Well, then, tell me about your retirement activity. You really seem to be enjoying yourself."

Here's what I told him. "For years, there were things

I'd wanted to do around the house that never seemed to get done. Now I have the time available. I recalled a technique that I'd used with great success in industry. I tried to accomplish at least one project or activity of major value each day. For many years, I even made a list of things I was going to do at the start of each day. My lists weren't long, just a few things I felt confident I could accomplish without letting routine things pile up. Using this approach, there was never any doubt in my mind as to what I had to do to achieve my goal for the day.

"After my retirement, I realized that if this approach worked for me in business, it could also work for me in retirement. I decided to apply the technique to writing and speaking. Since I made that decision, I haven't had a dull day of retirement. I've been totally happy because I'm either contacting someone about a speaking engagement, preparing a talk, or speaking before an audience. Every day, I set out to do at least one or two things I consider to be of real value, things I have made up my mind I want to accomplish."

"Bill," he said, "You've talked me into it. I'll call about that job first thing tomorrow."

"Why not right now?" I asked.

Moments later, he said, "Bill, I've got to get home now. It's been good talking with you. I'll call that company sometime tomorrow."

"Why don't you call them now?" I insisted.

He wrinkled his brow. "There's just not enough time left this afternoon. Besides, I've waited this long, another day won't matter all that much."

What Others Think of Our Name
— The Value of Integrity

I am absolutely convinced that there is a sure-fire method

of reducing a person's self-esteem and destroying the value of a person's name in his or her own eyes and in the eyes of others. Simply deny him or her the opportunity of challenge. Systematically deny that person the occasional need to cope with adversity, and you will produce an intellectual and moral weakling, totally incapable of greatness and devoid of initiative and self-reliance. This individual will devalue his or her name as a result. Consider this story.

A person that I at one time called a friend required surgery to have plastic veins placed in both legs. He was disabled and unable to work, and he was drawing a healthy social security benefit. He exercised properly, and after two years he could walk almost normally and was ready to return to work. He was offered a job, and I assumed he would take it. But one day I overheard him tell a mutual acquaintance, "No, I'm not going to take that job. I can't afford to work for only twenty dollars a week." I thought, "Well, those dirty bums, because of his physical handicap they are only offering him twenty dollars a week!" But when I investigated, I learned that he meant that he was not willing to work for only twenty dollars a week more take-home pay than he was drawing as tax-free social security. He's continuing to draw social security, and you and I are paying for it. The social security took away both his initiative and the integrity which I had once associated with his name.

Consider another story. We have a farm bureau in the county where I live. One of our farmers went in one day and told the clerk that he needed some rat poison. The clerk mentioned a specific type of poison. "I've tried that," the farmer said. "It didn't work." The clerk recommended a stronger poison. "I've tried that, too," the farmer said. "It's a little better than the first one you recommended, but it's still not good enough." When the clerk suggested a third and even stronger poison, the farmer complained that he had tried that also, but he was still overrun with rats.

The clerk excused himself to talk to the manager. While he was gone, another farmer came up and said, "Fella, I suggest that on your way out of town you stop at the Welfare Office and have them give you a bag of welfare flour. Take it home and feed it to those rats."

"I'll do anything," was the reply, "but will it kill the rats?"

"No," said the other farmer, "it won't kill them. But once those rats get a taste of that welfare flour, they'll just sit on their hindquarters and die of hunger waiting for you to bring them some more."

People who give no value to their name—those with such low self-esteem that they refuse to show initiative—do not encourage others to place much value on their name, either. If others are to think well of us and value our name highly, we must constantly build up our name by our *own* conscientious effort.

I'm told that one of the former governors of Kansas gave a talk about Abraham Lincoln. In his remarks, he observed that "Lincoln the underprivileged, Lincoln the rail-splitter—if he were alive today, he'd be receiving a federal subsidy for rail splitting. Some service organization would be providing him with good reading material. Still another service organization would provide him with an adequate reading lamp so he wouldn't harm his eyesight. A foundation would provide him with a scholarship to an institution of higher learning. The federal government would pay him a subsidy for growing a crop he was planning to grow anyway. And the Department of Agriculture would see to it that he was paid for not growing a crop he had no intention of growing. The result? There would be no Abraham Lincoln to remember."

Lincoln was faced with adversity, and through his own conscientious effort developed the integrity—the value of his name—for which we remember him.

The Value We Want Others to Place on Our Name — The Importance of Responsibility

Have you ever been in prison? Oh, you haven't? Well, I believe that you *have* been in prison. Don't take offense. I'm not calling you a liar. When I say prison, I'm not talking about penal institutions. I'm not talking about prisons made of mortar and brick and rock and steel. I'm talking about self-made prisons.

Consider the prison of ignorance—our failure to expose ourselves to a constant stream of new ideas, to books, cassettes, and other sources of enlightenment. Then there's the prison of procrastination—our preoccupation with the trivial and insignificant instead of attending to what we know in our heart and mind is best for ourselves and for those in our lives to whom we have responsibilities.

Then there's the prison where I confess I spend more time than I should—the prison of self-indulgence. Many of us are inmates of this institution. We'd rather play golf than visit with a lonely friend, or study current legislation so we can be an informed voter, or arrange for more adequate financing for ourselves and for the members of our family.

Inadequacy is a terrible prison. "Someone else can do the job so much better than I can." "If I had her experience, I'd be able to sign up all those real estate listings and make all those sales." "If I had his background, I'd be able to travel in the country club set, get all that business, and have all that influence."

But the worst prison of all is fear. In this prison, we are mentally maimed and psychologically crippled. We're afraid to attempt an important project because there's a chance it won't turn out just right, or someone may laugh at us. The fear of failure paralyzes us. We don't even *try* to make the sale, take the course, or tackle the project. Why? Because we're afraid our performance won't be up to snuff, that we'll look foolish in the eyes of our friends and family. If we're to realize the fullest value of our name, we've got to break out of all our prisons into God's glorious sunshine of freedom so we can be responsible for our own lives.

If we want others to value our names highly, we must learn to take responsibility for ourselves and our actions—we must responsibly and conscientiously try to enhance ourselves.

Speaking of breaking out of prison, have you ever seen an eagle fly? No other creature in the sky shows such stamina, so much strength, so much fortitude. An eagle in flight is truly a joy to behold: graceful, keen of vision; you can almost feel its strength as you watch it soar high above, seemingly without effort.

What makes this towering strength possible? The feathers, of course. And how do these feathers develop? One at a time. Very tiny plumes begin to grow—short, tender, flexible. As they grow into feathers, they become long and strong, and all of them together make the eagle's display of strength and power possible.

And isn't this how we become strong, how we learn, how we achieve our goals—a little at a time? We are the sum-total of all our small individual efforts to grow mentally as well as in body as we build the value of our name in the eyes of others.

Responsibility for the value of your name and for your success is totally yours. I learned this truism for myself in an interesting way.

182

Whenever we can, my wife and I slip away from our home and take mini-vacations. One of our favorite pastimes is visiting some of the many historic old Southern plantations now open to the public. If possible, we try to go in the middle of the week. That way, there will not be many other visitors and the hostess will be able to spend time talking with us.

In one of these beautiful old homes, my wife noticed a picture on the mantel in the living room, and she asked, "Whose picture is that?" "That's a picture of William Harrison," we were told. "Are you sure?" my wife asked. "That face looks very familiar." The hostess took the picture down, read a historical note on the back, and said, "Oh, I'm sorry. This is a picture of William Fitz-Hugh." "That's my husband!" my wife exclaimed. "I rather doubt that," the hostess explained, "because the note here says that, in 1663, the king of England granted seventeen thousand acres to this William Fitz-Hugh in Northern Virginia."

I started doing a lot of multiplying in my head. Seventeen thousand acres times the value of an acre of land in Northern Virginia is truly an astronomical figure. I had difficulty even placing the decimal properly. Suddenly, the value of my name shot way up.

Not too long after that, I was visiting a relative in Washington, D.C. As we were crossing the Potomac River into Virginia, I said, "You know, right over there where the Pentagon now stands, one of our ancestors—a certain William Fitz-Hugh by name—owned seventeen thousand acres of land back more than 200 years ago."

My relative smiled. "I know that. How much of the land do you own now?"

"None," I said.

"See, the family squandered it all," was my companion's reply. And the value of my name dropped a notch or two.

Some time later, this same relative returned from a trip to England. He advised me that, during the twelfth century, the king of England commented in the presence of his close friends, including a man named William Fitz-Hugh, that he wished the Archbishop of Canterbury did not exist. This William Fitz-Hugh recruited a few henchmen, and together they murdered the Archbishop in cold blood.

It took me a while to adjust to the idea that a relative of mine was a murderer. And the value of my name dropped another notch. Finally, I had to realize that the value of my name has nothing to do with the activities of my ancestors. The true value of my name, whether it be high or low, is entirely *my* responsibility, just as the true value of your name is *your* responsibility and no one else's.

The True Value of Our Name
— How It Helps Us

When you place a high value on your name, show integrity so others will think well of you, and take responsibility for your actions so you can help develop what others think of you, the true value of your name begins to work for you. Consider this story.

Some years ago, I had the privilege of working for a full day with one of the crack salesmen employed by our company. His name was Tom, and he was terrific. He was extremely well versed on our products, knew his territory—the Philadelphia area—inside and out, and understood his customers and their needs perfectly. In fact, he was so good that there was very little for me to do but stand by and watch. We had a very successful day.

When late afternoon drew near, we started to head back to the office to meet with the regional sales manager

184

and the rest of his staff. Before we did, however, Tom said to me, "Bill, would you make just one more call with me? It won't be a pleasant call, and I can assure you the customer won't greet us with open arms. He's one tough cookie." "That's all right," I said, "I'll be happy to go."

As we entered the reception room, every seat was filled with salesmen trying to see a purchasing agent. Tom presented our card to the receptionist. A short time later, this towering man—the buyer—walked into the room to see us. I was disappointed that he had not chosen to see us in his private office.

The buyer looked at my card and said, "Humph, vice president of sales. Tell me, how in the world did a guy like you ever get a job like that?"

I said, "Well, now that you ask me, I'll tell you. Our company employs many of the best sales professionals in the nation." I told the buyer about one of our men in Columbia, South Carolina, who had done a marvelous job. Because he performed so well for me, I looked great in the eyes of my company's top management. I remember telling him, "Charlie, when you and I were working together in the home office, you were so dedicated, so sincere, and so productive, you freed me to do other things. I had more time for personal attention to our major accounts."

Relating the story about Charlie gave me momentum, and I went on to tell the Philadelphia buyer about a number of other people in our organization. I wound up by talking about Tom, the salesman I was with. I said, "Do you know that all of the customers we visited today told me that, when they place their business in Tom's hands, they can forget their problems? They know that Tom will do everything within his power to honor his commitments and deliver as promised."

Now of course we didn't receive an order that day.

But the next morning as I was driving to Baltimore to spend the day working with another member of our sales team, I thought about that last Philadelphia buyer. That man was really trying to put me down in Tom's eyes. Tom had truly built a good reputation with that buyer and didn't recognize it. I stopped my car at the first available telephone booth and placed a call. "Tom," I said, "as a result of the value you have built into your name, that last buyer we talked to yesterday is anxious to place an order with you. He didn't want to give it to you in my presence because he didn't want the man from the home office to take credit for the sale. He knows the value you place on your name, and he values it also. He wants you to have the credit he thinks you deserve, and I know that, if you go back there today, you'll get a good-sized order."

Tom did go back, and he did get the order. Because he valued his name, others respected his integrity. Since that time, the buyer has become a lasting customer, and he and Tom have become good friends. As an interesting sidelight, Tom advised me recently that the buyer has now been promoted to—you guessed it!—vice-president.

Another incident in my business career reinforced my appreciation of the importance of other people in building the value of my name. At one time, the president of a competitive firm offered me the opportunity to work for his company. I told him I was both honored and flattered by the offer, but I couldn't accept it. A couple of months later, his son came to see me and renewed the father's offer. Once again I said I appreciated the offer but that I had to decline. At a still later time, the president of the competitive firm and I found ourselves at the same social function. He cornered me and once again I was offered a key position with his firm.

He complained that I was single-handedly responsible for wooing away many of his best customers to my employer's company. "That's not true," I said.

"That's what my people tell me," he replied.

"Well, they don't have all the facts. If I went to work for you," I continued, "you'd expect me to get all that lost business back for you. Isn't that so?"

"Of course I would," he said.

"The problem is," I explained, "that unless you hire all of the other people who have made my sales success possible—the president of our company, the vice president of traffic and transportation, and the other members of my support team, I couldn't do the job for you."

I was truly flattered, but this man had unrealistically inflated the value of my name by failing to consider that my success—and the success of our company—was the result of team effort. Here, the true value was in our *company* name.

Working to Build the Value of Our Name

In building the value of our name, we simply cannot respond passively to the challenges with which life presents us. Consider the tale of two frogs that fell into a bucket of cream. The bucket was deep, the sides were steep, and it was only half full. One of the frogs, due to the experience he had obtained during just a few short years of life, decided to accept his fate. He simply let events take their course. He did absolutely nothing. He drowned.

The second frog didn't know what to do either. But he decided to do what he could just to stay alive until he could think of some way out of his seemingly hopeless dilemma. As any frog can tell you, creatures of his kind are naturally gifted with strength in their legs; so he began to paddle, and paddle, and paddle, and paddle with all of his might. Well, would you believe it? A miracle?

187

The cream turned to butter and the frog jumped out. When faced with adversity, how hard do you paddle? How hard do you work to build the true value of your name?

On a recent vacation trip, my wife and I passed an old general store. Curious to see just what merchandise the proprietor stocked, we decided to spend a little time looking around. Much to our delight, we found many things similar to what had been stocked in the country store we went to as children. Toward the back of the store, we found a neglected collection of old and unusable items in a state of semi-storage and decay. On the wall was a yellowed, faded sign. I adjusted my glasses so I could read it more clearly. It said, "If you're at the end of your rope, we have more in stock." So many times during a person's day, we find ourselves at the end of our rope (and patience) with some other person or situation we're trying to deal with. Recognize that each of us has plenty of extra rope in stock. We're storing it up with the time we spend on self-improvement as we add to the value of our name.

The Value of Our Name
— The Value of Understanding

In closing, I want to tell you about the lovely valley in Virginia where I live, and the beautiful mountains on either side of my valley. Whenever I travel East, it's necessary to cross the Blue Ridge mountains. When I travel West, I have to cross the Alleghenys. Whenever I cross the top of these mountains, I am deeply moved by the panoramic view of the valley I call home. You can see for miles. What I feel, standing there on top of the mountain is—for me—a mountain-top experience.

Yet down in the valley below, work goes on as usual. Often, I think of how important it is for all of us to enjoy an occasional "mountain-top experience." We can and do have many such experiences in our lives. They enable us to go back to our own home valleys where we can live with renewed vigor and make a more positive contribution to our own lives and the lives of our neighbors. These experiences help us understand the innermost workings of our minds—the stuff of which the person who bears our name is made.

Clearly, we can't spend all of our time having mountain-top experiences; but we can use these moments to make ourselves better, more valuable human beings. Each of us, in our own minds, must decide on when and how often we will have a mountain-top experience. That is, to build the value of our name, we must take the time to understand ourselves.

I truly hope, as you ponder the value of your name from time to time, that it will prove to be a mountain-top experience for you. As I think about you, I am having a mountain-top experience. And when I return to my valley, I will have been enriched for having had the privilege of sharing these thoughts with you. God bless you.

PETER H. THOMAS

Peter Thomas is a dynamic young businessman, born in London, England, and living now in Victoria, British Columbia. He is having a most remarkable career. After leaving home at age 15, he joined the Canadian Army, where he finished his schooling and stayed for seven years. During this time, he did a tour of duty in the Middle East.

Upon his discharge, he tried several jobs: carpentry, sales clerk, and clerk in the oil patch. His oil field employer suggested he spend two years in Turkey on a contract, but since he had just gotten married and wouldn't be allowed to take his wife, he decided to look for other employment.

Peter obtained his first selling job as sales trainee for

a national investment company. He stayed with this company for five years and, during this time, broke every company sales record. He was top salesman, top branch manager, top regional manager, and finally general sales manager. During his third year of sales, in four months out of twelve he earned commissions of over $10,000 per month. Peter has earned many commissions in excess of $100,000 since then, his largest single commission being $325,000.

In 1968, he formed his own investment company. Since that time, he has built his corporation into one of the major real estate corporations in Canada.

Peter is chairman of the board for Century 21 Real Estate Ltd., Canada, a company whose sales exceed $1 billion per year. He is a member of the Board of Governors of St. Michael's University School. He was accepted as one of the youngest members of the Young President's Organization in Canada. And most important, he is a *salesman*!

You may contact Peter by writing to Samoth Financial Corporation Ltd., 1214-345 Quebec St., Victoria, B.C., Canada V8V 1W4, or by calling (604) 388-5123.

CRYSTALLIZING YOUR GOALS — STARTING NOW

by PETER H. THOMAS

"He who tries something and
fails is infinitely greater
than he who tries nothing
and succeeds."
        —Confucius

I know that you are interested in becoming even more successful than you are now, as you have already demonstrated by purchasing this book. Every chapter in this book can assist you in attaining your individual goals by sharing with you some proven tips from already successful people.

When I look back over my career, I have found that, although I have always had the drive to be successful, somehow I lacked the ability to sit down and write out my goals as they specifically related to my own personal objectives.

I am not speaking about writing out a list of priorities at the beginning of each day, week, or month, as I am assuming you are already doing that now. What I am speaking about is writing down, in a simple way, the values that are most important to you as an individual. Once you have your values set out in writing and have prioritized them, you will have absolutely no problem in setting your overall goals.

It will be from these overall goals, once they are written out in detail, that you will form your monthly, weekly, and daily priorities.

In my own life, I have found that the best method to assist me in remaining enthusiastic and motivated is to achieve. Of course, in order to measure achievement, one must have preset goals. Without goals, we wind up letting circumstances control us, instead of us controlling circumstances. As you well know, if you want to goof off, it is very easy to find many individuals who are available to goof off with. If you do not have specific goals written down, it is virtually impossible to measure your accomplishment, and of course you leave yourself wide open to rationalizing why you did not want to succeed anyway.

You always must remember that when I'm speaking about goals I'm speaking about your *own* goals, not goals that are forced upon you or are given to you by anybody else. Consequently, what I intend to do in this chapter is to assist you in every way possible to attain the goals that you have set. It is exceedingly important for you always to remember that the goals I speak of are your goals and yours alone. Another reason it is so difficult to establish priorities is that there are so many things that compete for your time. This is another reason for you to set down goals in writing so that you can reinforce them in your mind any time that you feel you are straying from them.

Unfortunately, most people experience the opportunity to reevaluate their lives, their goals, and their priorities only once in their lifetime—usually when they either come close to death themselves or lose a close friend. It is my objective in this chapter to give you an opportunity to do a soul-searching reevaluation without having to suffer any personal loss or anguish.

The first thing that you must do is take two or three pencils and an eraser together with a new pad of ruled 8½ inch by 11 inch paper and go by yourself somewhere that has an absolute minimum of distractions. I am speaking of a place where there is both beauty and solitude, such as your own very private place in the woods, possibly a location high on a hill overlooking a beautiful river, or even a very special place that you go to visit on your holidays.

When you are finally located in your very special place, you will find that, while the technique of checking your priorities is very simple, it requires the hardest work of all—the art of *pure thinking.* You must concentrate wholly on what you are doing. Do not allow your thoughts to wander. Just before you commit anything to writing on your paper, sit back and think about the most important person in your life—you. Think about the highlights and the most important events of your life so far, such as the day you graduated, the day you got married, the date your first child was born, the date you joined the military, the date you were discharged, the date you got your pilot's license, etc. Now list these important events on a sheet of blank paper.

You have now started into the difficult part of your assignment, and that is the art of pure thinking. At this stage, continue to think about yourself. Review your accomplishments thus far in your life. Fantasize and think about the future things that you want to attain. You will find your thoughts coming fast and furiously. Write all of these goals down fast and furiously, before you forget them. It is important at this stage not to stifle your thinking, because—remember—you can always rip up this page. These thoughts are for you and for you alone, and it is intended to get out on paper once and for all the fabulous and exciting dreams that you have either stored in your head or were really too embarrassed or not committed enough to pull from your head and put down on paper.

You now have in front of you a piece of paper that hopefully is filled up with various goals and objectives, and you are now ready for the second phase of this lesson in goal setting.

Take another piece of blank paper and write at the top "My Values." Do not concern yourself with priorities at this point. Simply list, in random order, such items as your business, your wife or husband, your children, your church, your financial assets, etc. On this page, just let your mind wander and write down everything that you can think of that you value personally.

Now take a third piece of paper and write at the top "My Values by Priority." Rank the values that are most important first, then put down the balance in descending order. On this page, list only your top eight to twelve values.

Take a fourth sheet of paper and write at the top "My Actions" for each of the values listed. Write down the specific actions that you have taken in the past year to support each of your values. What investment of energy, financial resources, or "quality time" have you made in each of the values that you place in high priority? If you can be objective with yourself, you will find some major discrepancies between your values and your actions.

Now start a fifth piece of paper and head it "My Values by Priority and Steps I Will Take This Year to See Them Accomplished or Furthered." It will be on this piece of paper that you are going to commit yourself to your goals—to the things that you will strive for this year in order to further the values that you have set out for yourself in the third page of this exercise.

You can continue with a sixth or seventh sheet to outline further what you are going to do to accomplish your priorities. You are now building an action program to invest your energy, your dollars, and your quality time into your highest values.

I hope that this session will just be a start. Most people find a day or two of solitude to complete this process is essential each year to keep focused on the things that they want to accomplish in life.

Good luck with setting your values. If you follow this simple formula, I know that it will dramatically change your life, as it has mine. It will give your life much more meaning, because everything you are doing becomes much easier when all your tasks help you get to where you want to go.

Sample Page One
MY GOALS AND OBJECTIVES

1. To lose 25 pounds

2. To become general sales manager
by better work performance

3. To take a holiday in Tahiti this year

4. To pay out my existing mortgage

5. To write a novel

Sample Page Two
MY VALUES

Health

Spouse

Family

Independence

Friends

Freedom

Respect of my colleagues and employees

Personal pride

Upgrading and general education

Self-respect

Sample Page Three
MY VALUES BY PRIORITY

1. My health

2. My freedom

3. Love and respect of spouse and family and the safety and continuation of the family unit

4. Self-respect

5. Upgrading of my general education

Sample Page Four
MY ACTIONS

1. Health
Maintained constant weight by eating properly and exercising daily. Joined a health club.

2. My freedom
Did not begin any projects or start any business relationships that would restrict or endanger my chosen life style.

3. The love and respect of my spouse and family and safety and continuation of the family unit
Took family for two week holiday at Christmas. Took son on a fishing trip, and went with spouse to Europe.

4. Respect of myself and people I admire
Managed all my affairs in a totally businesslike and honest manner. Treated everyone I came into contact with as I would like to be treated myself. Contributed financially and with personal time to my son's private school.

5. Upgrading of my general education
Read several books. Took a speed reading course. Took flying lessons and attended all training sessions. Attended an education conference.

Sample Page Five
MY VALUES BY PRIORITY
AND STEPS I WILL TAKE
THIS YEAR TO SEE THEM
ACCOMPLISHED OR FURTHERED

1. Health:

Maintain a daily minimum exercise program.
Keep informed of all recreation courses.
Swim at least two days per week.
Keep weight chart.

Walk whenever possible.

Spend lots of quiet time to reassess my
health program.

2. Freedom:

Total freedom is nothing more than
absolute discipline.

Build my personal assets and revalue my
net worth on a monthly basis.

When making commitments always calculate what
the worst is that could happen and if that is
not acceptable, DON'T make the commitment.

Sample Page Five
(Continued)
MY VALUES BY PRIORITY
AND STEPS I WILL TAKE
THIS YEAR TO SEE THEM
ACCOMPLISHED OR FURTHERED

3. Self-Respect:

Contribute meaningfully to my favorite organization, which includes volunteer work.

Do not use any profanity in the coming year.

Never pass on a rumor, hearsay, or innuendo.

Become more knowledgeable with respect to government politics.

4. My Family:

Set aside specific times for me to be with them individually and together.

Each month, evaluate time spent with family members. Insist on picnics, island tours, hikes, etc.

Plan annual holiday with my spouse.

LOLA GREEN

A multi-faceted background with expertise in conference planning and an extraordinary understanding of people all combine to make Lola Green truly an outstanding innovator in her field. Her very special spunk, humor, drive, and talent work together to create a really exciting and magnetic personality—one that's worth watching.

After graduating from Cornell University, Lola criss-crossed her way through Europe where she acquired her first-hand knowledge of outstanding vacation hideaways and began her coverage of travel spots for the magazine media back home. Upon returning to the U.S., she worked in the field of special education, designing programs for a residential medical center for emotionally disturbed children. She then became responsible for developing and operating a career guidance program for unwed mothers and subsequently founded a nutritional educational center in Long Island, New York.

Having caught the "travel bug," Lola's dream was to publish a book on exotic vacation resorts by the seaside, and she set out to see if she could make it a reality. With persistence and determination, Lola's dream became a reality when she was commissioned by one of the world's largest corporations to write a book on elegant vacation spots for lovers of the sea, and the book *Great Places by the Sea* became a hit overnight!

Besides her travel interests, Lola has been speaking to groups all over the country in the areas of communication skills, decision-making, self-esteem, and creativity. Her program entitled "How to Live with a Busy Executive" is especially successful with spouse audiences. Speaking from first-hand experience (she is the wife of the president and chairman of the board of the nationwide network of Harrison Executive Conference Centers), Lola finds this program has a very positive carryover to the personal as well as the business life of a husband-wife team. Lola is the mother of twin boys, thus rounding out the picture of the emerging woman of today—wife, mother, and career woman.

You may contact Lola by writing to her at Program Innovators, Lattingtown Road, Glen Cove, N.Y. 11542, or telephoning (516) 671-5150.

CREATING YOUR OWN "LUCKY BREAKS"

by LOLA GREEN

What if you were brought up in an environment where you were:

- Taught that one of the most critical things in life was to probe and explore your own innate talents and interests.

- Given supportive help and encouragement in helping you choose what you wished to do in life.

- Helped out when you got in over your head.

- Looked upon and treated as though you had a special kind of uniqueness that was adored and respected.

- Surrounded by people who were genuinely happy for you when you got what you were after.

If this is the environment you were given, you were a very lucky soul indeed. Most of us were not so fortunate. But that doesn't mean that the rest of our lives must be shortchanged because circumstances didn't provide us with the nurturing we needed as children. It took me many years to realize that you can correct this early omission by becoming aware of your own uniqueness and by tapping into your personal style, since only from that source can your energy and creativity flow.

Self-Destructive Myths

Part of the problem for many of us is that we are raised with a couple of false notions that are destructive to our growth. First is the myth that we must always win at everything. Why is it that we can't just enjoy instead of focusing on the winning? Why do we always have to be the best at *everything* we do? Do you ever actually remember whether you won a particular tennis match four days after it's over? If winning is absolutely essential to you, and particularly when it comes to exercise you participate in for relaxation, there is plenty of evidence to indicate that you are only adding more stress and tension to your life and that some day you will likely be confronted with that one time forever final coronary attack! I am not condemning competition. It's only bad when it becomes an obsession in your life style, when, rather than enjoying the process of living, you only want to "win, win, win."

The second myth tells us to play down our own assets—almost to the point of deprecation. This is a problem that is particularly acute for most women. Just take a quick test right now. Close your eyes and ask yourself what one word best describes your appearance. If you are female, generally the first word that comes to mind is something negative. Maybe it's not terribly negative but just not very positive. Very few of us are likely to say something unabashedly complimentary of ourselves. Our Puritan heritage has taught us to be self-effacing. There is still the sinister suspicion that it is shameful to have a fierce pride in oneself and in one's strengths. We are taught that it is charming, enchanting, and modest to put ourselves down. Baloney!

Take, for example, the last time you were complimented—whether it was on your appearance, your accomplishments, or whatever. Were you able to accept it graciously? And equally important, did you believe it? Or did something inside of you say, "If he only really knew the truth!" So an important rule is: Never put yourself down.

The Need for Self-Acceptance

The reason we frequently put ourselves down, and the reason most of us have trouble accepting compliments, is because we don't feel worthy of compliments. We simply do not like ourselves very much. Not only do we not care for ourselves, but we don't really know ourselves. What we end up doing is internalizing impressions of ourselves from everyone out there rather than honestly coming to grips with all the personal potential we each possess. When we both know and like ourselves, we have self-acceptance.

How do we establish a blueprint for self-acceptance and with it the happiness it brings? In striving to meet our fullest potential, it is important to remember that we can reach our goal only after our basic needs have been met (i.e., food, shelter, and safety). Abraham Maslow, one of the most eminent psychologists of our time, described what he called a "hierarchy of needs" which had to be met before a person could attempt to fill the need to create or become self-actualized. He said, basically, that we first must have our physical needs met in order to survive. After this, we need a sense of belonging, a feeling we have some power over our lives and a sense of being recognized for our own uniqueness. In short, it is difficult for a hungry person to be concerned with reaching out to explore his or her talents and form meaningful relationships with others. Hungry people first need to be concerned with getting food on the table. But many of us who are well-fed, well-housed, and safe have stopped developing once we obtained these basic needs. To gain self-acceptance, one must take the risks involved in trying to do things differently. We must develop a sense of newness about how we approach life.

The Importance of Risk-Taking

Today, we know there is an increased emphasis on "doing your own thing." There is much more opportunity for self-determination, particularly for women. We are freer to discover our own talents, interests, and personal goals. We are able to move towards them without being stifled by rigid tradition and custom. This new sense of freedom and choice doesn't necessarily make life easier because it brings with it the need to understand oneself, to crystallize one's own life goals, and to make decisions. An important ingredient of my success came with the realization that risk-taking is a necessary part of life if you wish to grow and expand as a human being. Risks are often viewed as kind of scary by most people. Obviously you don't plunge in where you are totally ignorant and take on things for which you are totally unprepared. But you never really know enough. In my judgment, the willingness to take risks is critical.

To illustrate my point, when I graduated from Cornell, with a major in Child Development and Family Relationships, I was hit with the reality of "where do I go from here?" The safest and easiest option would have been to stay in New York, find a job there, and rely on my parents to pave the way financially until I found my direction. I chose instead to head on to Boston (where I literally knew no one) with a suitcase and a bit of pocket money, realizing that if I wanted that independence I so earnestly sought, I had to make it on my own. I remember vividly arriving in Boston by Greyhound bus and heading over to the student housing office at Harvard University in Cambridge so I could find myself a roommate and a place to plant myself until I found a job. Crossing off dozens of phone numbers one by one, I came upon a perfect situation five blocks from the telephone booth I was standing in. Within fifteen minutes, I found myself in an old brownstone that was to become my home for the next year. I took a risk to become independent; taking the risk taught me a great deal about myself and particularly about independence.

Understanding Independence

Living in Boston, I learned in a few months that independence and needing people are not inconsistent with each other. The fact is (except perhaps in the case of some hermits), there is no such thing as total independence. If you're looking for it, you're looking for a myth. Independence is being free and able to rely on your own resources to cope with the world but flexible enough to seek help when you need it. Not only do all of us have dependency needs, but to deny this in ourselves actually diminishes us and the ones we love. To be accused of being a dependent person has become an insult in our culture to the

211

extreme where needing someone is viewed as a sign of weakness. Most of us enter marriage thinking there isn't a thing we can't share with or ask of our mate. Somewhere along the way, many of us have come to look on it as dependency to turn for emotional help to the person who is closest to us, even though we would never dream of considering it "dependency" to call in an electrician or a carpenter. Indeed, this negative attitude about the word "dependency" seems to be a growing way of life in marriage in the United States—a phenomenon that's showing up increasingly in the ever-growing divorce rate in our country.

Why this stigma on "dependency"—particularly in the marriage relationship? I believe that people who really feel secure are able to accept their normal dependencies. But when they feel inadequate, they feel it's "degrading" to have to reach out for help. The ideal relationship, in my opinion, includes being both dependent and independent, which adds up to "interdependence." I am, for instance, completely dependent on my husband in certain areas of my life and completely independent in others. And he is exactly the same with me. My husband travels a great deal, as do I, and we have learned to live with the solitude and aloneness when the other one is gone, and yet our lives are so woven together that there are certain things I couldn't conceive of doing without him. Keep remembering that in life what you're seeking is a relationship of genuine mutuality, of self-acceptance and acceptance of each other as individuals, and that you can't ever really be independent as long as you're not even independent enough to ask for help! If your life is not all you wanted, you can blame yourself, or blame circumstances, or get all the help you need and change it.

It's important to remember that, in working towards whatever goals you set for yourself in life, the chances of getting what you want are always better if those around you are also getting what they want—especially when it comes to others who are significant in your life.

So in my family we have set aside a special night for all of us to sit together and talk about what is important to us individually and as a family. We call this special night "Family Night," and it is a practice we have maintained for several years. It is a meaningful night for us, since it is a time to share all our joys and disappointments, our gripes, and our successes with each other. I believe that families are held together by the things they jointly dream about, plan for, and do with each other. There is something of a ritual about the family night, a sense of renewing things in common. It is a time to learn more about each other through the reactions that are given to what we felt about the week that went by and a deepening respect for each other's point of view. I would eagerly recommend that you consider having such a family night once a week in your home, if you don't already have one. It truly promotes a sense of oneness and harmony that I believe will remain as a buffer against later misunderstandings.

How Do You Make "Lucky Breaks"?

As time has unfolded, I have developed a handful of beliefs that are central, I think, to those "lucky breaks" I have enjoyed. One of the first is the importance of self-confidence. You have to give the impression of being confident in your abilities and comfortable with who you are and where you're going. I have learned to view myself as intelligent, creative, articulate, and able to be of value to other people. It may sound conceited, but if you don't view yourself that way, why should anyone else? You have to know who you are and be willing to go after what you want in life.

Consider this experience of mine. When I was graduating from high school, I was a very self-conscious and awkward young lady. I vividly remember the day in late spring when I received the college acceptance letter from the school of my choice, Cornell University. As I opened the thick white packet with my acceptance letter and registration information, I was torn between disbelief and hysteria: I had never believed that I could be accepted to the college of my choice in spite of my good grades in high school. My disbelief was so acute, I can remember calling up the dean's office at Cornell to ask if there was a mistake. "Had the computer entered the wrong name by accident?" I meekly asked the dean. I was then promptly told that indeed the college had accepted me and they were thoroughly convinced I could make it—now all that was necessary was my own conviction that I could! This was one of my first confrontations with realizing that being able to succeed depends not upon the absence of self-doubt but on the ability to go ahead in the presence of self-doubt!

Taking Things into Your Own Hands

I suppose the decision I made in my professional life about which I agonized the most and had the worst doubts and terrors was one of the smartest things I ever did. It revolved around my decision to pull my travel guide book out of the "waiting pool" at a top publishing house, after futilely waiting two years for the editor-in-chief to give the go-ahead with a contract. The agony of not having a definitive yes or no seemed to last an eternity, and I finally made the decision to take things into my own hands and pull that book out of this elite publishing house and sell the book on my own to a major corporation. Getting published, as anyone who has been in the business can tell you, is not an easy task! Well, to my amazement, three weeks later, I had created for myself that long-awaited contract and received a commission from the world's largest corporation, A.T.&T., for many thousands of books. My travel guide was to become a reality! How did all this happen? Simply through a lot of hard work governed by cool, logical thoughtfulness, persistence, and determination.

Decision-Making

Another important competence which I believe makes for "lucky breaks" and successful living is the ability to make decisions expediently. The mistakes of inaction are always likely to be worse than mistakes of genuine impulse. We all know people who go through the agonies of indecision before taking any important step. There are always going to be arguments either for or against something. Sometimes, the more we think about them, the more they work against each other, until sometimes we end up in an irritable state of paralysis. Nobody ever really feels they know everything they ought to know before making a decision. At some point, you have to come to grips with the fact that "I know as much as I can in my present state of awareness and now I must act." And all of us who have postponed a decision because we were fearful that we didn't know enough have subsequently found out that more time frequently doesn't alter the decision. There comes a time when you have to say, "I really don't know enough but I've done what I can to learn as much as I'm able to about this problem and now I must make a decision." At the time of any decision, your awareness is helping you to make the best decision you can. Now this doesn't mean there are no doubts. It simply means that you're prepared to go ahead in the face of the doubts.

The problem of acquiring skill in making decisions is especially acute for women, and there is a tremendous feeling of anxiety, confusion, frustration, and uneasiness because their experiences have not prepared them for decisions. Many people are not even aware of the number of choices they could make in a given situation and some feel better letting others make choices for them.

Indeed, most people, men or women, have had little practice or help in learning how to make well-informed, well-considered choices in life. Yet we are all constantly being told or asked to decide on so many things. Practice in learning and applying decision-making skills would undoubtedly help you with some of your difficulties in this area.

Self-Examination

A good beginning in gaining greater freedom of choice and control over your life is to examine some of your attitudes towards yourself because what people think of themselves has a great deal to do with what decisions they make. So to begin with, start to get more in tune with knowing yourself, what is important to you, what you can do now, and what your short-range and long-range objectives are. It is essential that you know what you want to do and that you figure out the kinds of skills you have and try to apply them to a job or a life goal. Finally, develop a plan of action or strategy for attaining what you want in life.

I love being around results-producing people. Yet I have come to realize I get into trouble when I confuse my desire for results (my desire for being acknowledged by others) with my sense of who I am, my self-worth, or my contentment in just living. Similarly, I cut off my capacity to appreciate and feel intimacy with others when I confuse who they, as individuals, are with the results they have produced in their lives.

Most importantly, in the past few years, I have learned the value and the enjoyment that come from linking people together. Most successful people have a network of people that they deal with professionally. They share with them and thus give meaning to their work.

For example, one of the most important groups for me has been an organization called the National Speakers Association. It is a committed network of speakers across the country providing a criss-crossing of communication lines that allows members to trade ideas, keep current with new developments in the speaking industry today, and end the deadly sense of isolation that so often envelops someone in our profession. At the annual convention held every year around the country, we attend a number of different workshops related to our profession and in this way we trade ideas and hook into lines of communication with one another. I meet people with whom I can bounce around ideas, try out different things, and just be creative and imaginative. Another wonderful aspect of this association is that there is a great deal of good influence from the top achievers in our industry. And I have found that the higher up you are in any profession and the more excited you are about what you do, the more eager and willing you are to explore with people and share your struggles, disappointments, and secrets to success. So another part of creating those "lucky breaks" and developing your personal and professional ability is to join professional associations in your field.

The Skill of Accomplishment

Let's talk a bit about accomplishments and their connection with "lucky breaks." Is it true that "it's not what you know but who you know" or that "being in the right place at the right time" is critical to success? Many accomplished people attribute their extraordinary achievements solely to good breaks or to casual fortuitous circumstances when in actuality their good fortune was the result of practicing certain skills consciously or unconsciously. As I see it, these skills can be translated into personal and professional preparation as you position yourself wisely. This, in my judgment, is what separates successful people from those who wait for success to happen!

All of the accomplishments I have earned have come through sheer drive and determination. Yes, luck and contacts occasionally help, but when "push comes to shove," it's what you're willing to do with the opportunities out there that will determine your success level.

It has been my own experience and the experience of successful people I've studied that you do not have to wait for someone else to give you that "lucky break." Just go out and create it for yourself!

Reflecting on my own career and how I got where I am, my accomplishments have been the result of a combination of planning, trying to identify opportunity, and being ready and eager to capture it when I see it.

By doing lots of research, thinking creatively, planning down to the last detail, it is quite possible for anyone to achieve almost any given task or project. Most importantly, I have learned how to make the most of the opportunities that chance offers. My advice to you is to just go out and grab them when you recognize them. So when the next opportunity appears on the horizon, just be ready to seize it.

The Importance of Self-Esteem

Let me leave you with one last thought. If you need help in the area of self-esteem, start reading several of the excellent self-help books readily available across the country. Better yet, enroll in a self-esteem program. I can almost guarantee that participating in such a program will add immeasurably to your joy of living. I highly recommend a program offered by the McGrane Institute in Cincinnati, Ohio, and presented by a loving and gifted human being named Bill McGrane. This program is offered once a month throughout the year, and you must commit yourself to an entire weekend to attend. It is a program that helped me immeasurably in my zest for living. I feel I have been given a special gift by participating in this program and so I pass it on to you so that you may share in the special dimension that such a program can add to your life. This kind of training simply accelerates our ability to love and accept ourselves while opening the channels to richly creative reservoirs.

If my message has touched you with the positive energy and the capacity to love that I feel, then we have truly communicated. Hopefully, you will now chance a look inside and discover for yourself all the dazzling possibilities you have within you and realize that you're sitting on the threshold of a great life adventure.

CHARLES E. "TREMENDOUS" JONES

One of the most dynamic and respected speakers our country has produced in 50 years, Charles E. "Tremendous" Jones entered the sales field at age 22. Within 10 years, his sales exceeded $10 million.

Charles is president of Life Management Services, Inc., and is a full-time motivational lecturer and consultant. His book, *Life Is Tremendous*, sold more than 100,000 copies during the first year of publication.

His speeches on leadership and life have spellbound more than 2,000 audiences from coast to coast as he punches home his points by helping his listeners to laugh at problems and failures, which, he insists, are actually stairsteps to success.

You may contact "Mr. Tremendous" by writing Life

Management Services, Inc., P.O. Box 1044, Harrisburg, PA 17108, or telephoning (717) 232-8562.

THE PRICE
OF LEADERSHIP

CHARLES E.
"TREMENDOUS" JONES

I know of no man who feels fully qualified to speak on the subject of leadership. In fact, it seems that those who appear to be the most qualified are often the most reluctant. Knowing that I am a student of the word, rather than an authority, I think my attitude toward what I'm about to say can best be described by the story of the young minister preparing to give his first sermon. As he read and observed, he could see so clearly everyone's mistakes, and he knew it would be simple to set everyone straight. He could hardly wait for the big day when he would be able to lower the boom on the congregation. Finally, the big day came, and he climbed to the pulpit for the great occasion. After speaking for a few minutes, he realized he was in trouble and began to sense that maybe

223

he wasn't the hope of the world. After a few more minutes, be began to wish that he'd never heard of preaching, and that there were a trap door behind the pulpit, so he could press a button and quickly slip out of sight. Of course there wasn't, and finally, after five minutes which seemed to be hours, he said a hasty benediction. Head hanging, he left the pulpit, discouraged, broken, and beaten. As he walked to the rear, an old white-haired war-horse slipped his arm over the boy's shoulder and said, "Son, if you'd gone up like you came down, you could have come down like you went up."

Leadership is, without a doubt, one of the most misunderstood and misrepresented words in our vocabulary. As a child, you may have never sought the definition of the word, but you didn't have to live very long before you discovered the satisfaction of being first and the heartache of being last. You also discovered that, while you didn't always have to be first, you could refuse to be last, because there always were so many who didn't seem to care. The person with only an ounce of competitive spirit is a most gifted individual. If you have at least that ounce of spirit, you can begin to look for the key to leadership. Once I began to look, I soon discovered that there are many leadership cults, most of which fall into three categories.

First, there is the *personality cult.* This group places the emphasis on looking the part, talking the part, acting the part, and you'll *be* the part. Members of this cult tell themselves all day long how great they are, but flop because they never attempt anything.

We all know people who look like what we think a leader should look like, and even though they have learned to look like a leader, talk like a leader, and act like a leader, they still aren't any more of a leader than they were when they began to develop that great leadership personality.

Next is the *title cult*. Members of this group think they aren't great because they don't have the title, position, power, or authority. They are the ones who burn out their lives to get the title, to be the leader, yet when they finally get the title, they find that no one would follow them anyway.

Finally, there is the *endowment cult*. This group has members who hang their heads, saying, "Some have, some don't—me, I ain't got it!" They are convinced of failure before they begin; they believe that only the luckily endowed can succeed.

Well, I may not have discovered or learned all that leadership is as yet, but I am sure of what it isn't. It is not personality, although it helps. It is not title or position, although it helps. It isn't endowment, although it helps. You ask, well, if it isn't any of these, what is it?

Leadership is a *price,* and it can be paid by anyone, any time, anyplace. You are as much of a leader today as you are going to be, because the price you are paying by your actions today is determining the kind of leader you will be tomorrow. You often hear that the wise person is preparing for his next job. While that statement may be sound, he or she had better be preparing by knowing and doing the best on the job at hand, or there may not be a next job. You should know that everyone has the privilege and obligation to lead in something. There is no one who can't lead in something, even if it's in mistakes. Even if you lead in mistakes, you'll wind up far better off than the poor wretch who would never dare anything. A failure is not a complete flop. At least failures serve as bad examples for others.

Now if leadership is a price, of what does the price consist? Like all the best things in life, leadership can be paid for by anyone with what they have inside themselves. I'm sure there are many things that could be added to my list, but experience has taught me that the price of leadership is *loneliness, weariness, abandonment,* and *vision.*

Loneliness

The price of leadership begins with *loneliness.* What is leadership? What does a leader do? A leader is simply one who goes ahead, sets the pace, and paves the way—alone. You must be willing to go forward alone—willing, and not necessarily able. There are many who are able but not willing, and it is the task of the willing to go ahead and do the job when those who are capable but unwilling refuse. Many people never arrive simply because they never start. Once a person decides to set the pace and move ahead, he or she discovers why some refuse to pay the first price of leadership. It's lonely leading. So many return to the pack to lead with the gang, only to discover too late that the gang isn't going anywhere.

Paying the first price of leadership begins with a *decision.* Another phrase we often hear: "I won't go ahead until I know I'm right." Seems strange how slowly we realize how many times the very things that appeared so wrong turned out so right, and the things that appeared so right turned out so wrong. I've come to the conclusion that we won't know for sure what is the right method or the wrong method until the end, and the end is a long way off. A man must decide to act, to get on with the show, or his most tremendous dreams and ambitions will profit him nothing. Consider the three facets of decision-making:

1. *Make it.* You've got to make your decision and follow it with more and more decisions. Remember those who never get started; they pay a price—each day of their

lives—for a pitiful reward. Don't second-guess yourself forever. Believe your beliefs, doubt your doubts, and get on with it.

2. *Make it yours.* There is nothing wrong with sound counsel or advice, but when paying the price of leadership, who understands your problem better than you? Who has risked his life on the decision except you? Many ideas never get off the ground because they are talked over with the wrong person. If you have to talk it over with someone, do it with someone you know who has already paid the price. In my own experiences, I've found many who want to talk things over with someone in order to be discouraged from starting.

I remember many times during my twelve years in management talking to someone about the tremendous career of selling. One of the most satisfying things I know is helping someone enjoy the rewards that we know. As I would be building up to a great climax, telling about the prestige, security, wealth, and happiness, the person's eyes would begin to light up and the smile would broaden. Then I'd pop the question, "What do *you* think?" Almost invariably the response was something like, "Tremendous!" Of course, I'd respond with a pen and contract, only to be greeted by an emphatic, "Wait!" And then the person would ask for time to talk it over with husband or wife. Now I think individuals should make decisions for themselves when their lives are being affected. When I get to be 65, I may be the biggest flop the world has ever known, but I'm going to get all the credit.

3. *Make it work.* Stick by your decision, die by it, never give up. We need to burn the word "stickability" into our hearts. There is an epidemic sweeping most communities. It's known as the quitters disease. Everywhere I go I hear the phrase, in many different tones, "I quit! I quit! I quit!"

227

The problem with most people is they don't realize what the problem is. I remember how I always wanted to quit. In fact, that's why I worked so hard to become successful, so that I wouldn't have to go through that agonizing wanting to quit all the time. Then, finally, I became a success, and to my surprise, I still wanted to quit. I then learned that the human being hits psychological lows two or three times a year, and wants to quit for no reason at all. Of course, the real problem was in wanting to quit because the more I wanted to quit, the more I wanted to quit; and the more I wanted to quit, the more afraid I was that I was going to quit. And I didn't want to quit, I just wanted to want to quit. Finally, one day I discovered the difference between quitting and wanting to quit. I then decided I would never quit, and now I enjoy quitting all the time, because I know I'm not going to quit. Sometimes someone will ask, "You mean you can't ever quit?" That's right. You can die, retire, or get fired, but that's it. Of course, there are exceptions, and you are going to think you're one of them every time you want to quit, but if you sell out that easily, you'll never manage to pay the first price of leadership. After you get your degree under your belt, go ahead and quit, or after you've built a great agency and are set for life and you want to walk away with nothing, go ahead. I think you'll agree that more is to be gained by stickability than by chasing better deals, when most of the time our attitudes at the time of our quitting set the stage for almost certain failure in the next job, too.

After you make your first decision, you are constantly confronted with decisions, but there are only a few that really count. While there may be more than life's three great decisions, I've found that once these are made, the rest are rather simple.

1. *Who will you spend your life with?* It is often said that a happy marriage is based on compatibility, among other things. While compatibility may be of help, the key to a successful marriage is the integrity of the decision made by two people to accept each other, for better or for worse (worse if necessary), for richer or poorer (poorer if necessary), until death do they part. That settles that. The only thing in question is their ability to make a decision, make it theirs, and make it work. A happy marriage was never the case of how much can two people get from each other, but rather a long learning process of how to give to each other.

2. *What job will you live your life in?* Some think that a work relationship is different than a marriage. If it is, I can't figure out how. A job demands the person love, honor, cherish, and obey, or it will not reward him or her with happiness. Some think that a job is a stepping stone to something better. There isn't anything better than what we have in our hands right now. Honor it, and it will be what you are looking for. We make it; it can't make us. We are its master. Vocational happiness is not determined by how much I can get out of it, but rather how much I can discover there is in me by allowing my involvement and commitment to bring it out in me. One of the key words in success is *control.* Control takes years to build and comes only to those who know what job they are going to live their lives in.

3. *What will you live your life for?* At a management meeting several years ago, Fred Smith asked a question that caused my ears to perk up: "What do you want written on your tombstone?" At first, I thought I'd need a huge monument to get it all on. His point was, however: What are you living your life for?

If you don't know, then how can you plan it? There

are only two ways to go, no neutral ground: *my way* or *God's way.* My purpose is not to preach to you, but simply to point out that most men think some things take care of themselves, and they never do. God is very real, always has been, always will be. The leader doesn't wait for trouble or death to become acquainted with the Author and Finisher of our faith. The leader is not interested in the errand-boy type of God that so many seek. The leader wants simply to know the truth and is confident the truth will enable him to live above circumstances and have a readiness of reserve for all who are looking to and leaning on him.

Weariness

This is the age of relaxation—take it easy; slow down; pace yourself, you'll live longer; be careful, you'll burn yourself out. I wasn't in the harness too long before I began to hear these popular phrases. One I recall was, "You've got to have a *hobby.*" With my work, family, and church, I couldn't understand why, because if I had twice the time, I couldn't do half as much as I wanted to. Sometimes I'd hear, "You've got to get away from it all." That's strange—I'm trying to get *into* it all. The leader learns that the sense of responsibility comes only to a few, and if your church, community, or company is to go on, you must carry the load that you and you alone can carry. You can give up when you want, but remember, no one can pay your price for you.

There is one thing that makes leading wearisome. The leader is constantly growing, and growth causes growing pains. Often growth comes only through failure. The young fellow asked the old timer how he became successful, to which the old timer replied, "Good judgment." The young fellow then asked, "How did you get that?" The old timer replied, "Experience." The young fellow asked again, "How did you get that?" And the old timer concluded, "Poor judgment."

Another wearisome phrase the leader often hears: "It isn't worth it." Of course it isn't. Who said it was? The leader is learning that he lives not a life of choice, but of necessities. He finds so often that he must do what has to be done, not what he wants to do. The leader often finds it wearisome when he tries to do the impossible. He finds the new approach where the old won't work. He has heard that you can lead a horse to water and can't make him drink, but you can put some salt in his oats and make him thirsty. The leader also never escapes those thoughtful souls who are always on the sidelines, telling him how he ought to be doing what they refuse to do.

Abandonment

There just isn't time to do all you want to do and all you should do. The leader is constantly learning to abandon the things that come naturally, like discouragement. Discouragement is, without a doubt, the most expensive luxury a man can afford. I believe the real mark of a great leader, or perhaps I should go further and say, the only success formula that I've ever seen that cannot fail is, "Be ye thankful." That is, instead of being discouraged, be thankful. Paul Speicher once said it another way: "An attitude of gratitude flavors everything you do." Thankfulness is the sign of the big man; thanklessness is the sign of the little man. Are you the most thankful person you ever met? If you aren't, *why* aren't you? Remember, you'll never be thankful for everything until you learn to be genuinely thankful for nothing. To learn to be thankful for the privilege of being thankful is one of the marks of greatness. The leader abandons the habit of getting in

231

order to be sharing. He knows that you never get to truly keep anything until you give it away. The cynic will cry out that this is not for our age, that he knows men who have all they ever got. What he can't see for his blindness is that they don't have what they acquired, it has them—what a difference!

It is easy for us to teach abandonment to others, but the leader knows the price of abandonment, beginning with his own thought processes. What do you think about? Let's go a step further. What do you talk about? Someone once said that little people talk about things, medium-sized people talk about people, and big people talk about ideas. Which kind of people do you like to be around? How are your reading habits? How many books have you read this year? How many are you reading now? How many of the ideas you've received from the books have you shared? The power of a single book at the right time in a man's life is unlimited. The leader leads the way, showing that leaders are readers. You should not only keep a flow of books for yourself, but give them away. Paperbacks are inexpensive and popular. It was Mac McMillon whom I first heard say, "You are today what you'll be five years from now, except for the books you read and the people you meet."

Vision

No person can pay the price of leadership without knowing where he is going and what he is doing. How easy it is to lay out what we want, but how difficult to find the real pathway to it. Perspective is so vital. The Scriptures have expressed it perfectly in: "Where there is no vision, the people perish." Certainly, this is multiplied for the leader. I think that, if I could have one wish granted, I'd ask that I be permitted to see clearly for ten minutes a day. If that could be done, the world would beat a path to my door because even the saints have had to look through a glass darkly. One of the most exciting thoughts that ever came into my mind was the discovery of what vision really is. I had thought perhaps it was unusual imagination or creativity. No, and as in all things, the best things are all at our feet, free and ready to be put to use. Vision is *being able to see things as they are.* I think much is gained by studying the people whose lives have stood the test of time, the men who saw things as they really were. Lincoln was a man of vision. One of his many great quotations hangs in my office: "I have been driven many times to my knees by the overwhelming conviction that I had nowhere to go—my own wisdom and that of all about me seemed insufficient for that day." Lincoln has taught me that no man ever truly grows up until he learns to go down. Daniel Webster was a man of vision. He was asked once what he considered the most important thought that ever entered his mind, to which he replied, "My personal accountability to Almighty God." Webster knew that every person, some day, stands for judgment, to give an account, and his account was in the hands of a Lawyer who has never lost a case. Patrick Henry was a man of vision. His spine-tingling speech, "Give me liberty or give me death," attests to this. The reason Patrick Henry could shout this with conviction is revealed in his last will and testament, where he writes, "My most cherished possession, I wish I could leave you, my Faith in Jesus Christ, for with Him and nothing else, you can be happy, but without Him and all else, you'll never be happy." Roger Hull closed an address with, "A man can be born with ability, he can acquire knowledge, he can develop skill, but wisdom comes only from God." We all need wisdom to be parents, citizens, employers, and employees. There is no place to buy wisdom, no school that teaches it, no course that offers it. No man can lead who doesn't know how to follow or who to follow. Where will we get our wisdom? Who are we following? How is our vision?

We began with a story to illustrate my approach to this subject. I'd like to close with a similar story which will sum up all I've tried to say. Once there was a boy rowing an old timer across a wide river. As the boy rowed on, the old timer picked a leaf from the water. He studied it for a while, and then asked the boy if he knew anything about biology, to which the boy replied, "No." The old timer said, "Son, you've missed 25% of your life." As they rowed on, the old timer took a rock from the bottom of the boat, and as he held it in his hand he asked the boy, "Son, do you know anything about geology?" The boy sheepishly replied, "No, sir, I don't." The old timer said, "Son, you've missed 50% of your life." As they rowed on, the twilight came and the old timer began to study the north star that had begun to twinkle. After a while, he asked the boy, "Son, do you know anything about astronomy?" The boy, with head low and embarrassed, replied, "No, I don't, sir." The old timer quickly and forcefully said, "Son, you've missed 75% of your life." Just then the boy noticed out of the side of his eye the huge dam upstream beginning to crumble and the water pouring over in torrents. Quickly he turned to the old timer and shouted, "Sir, do you know how to swim?" The old timer replied, "No." The boy shouted back, "You just lost your life!"

A man may not know all the methods and techniques, he may not be the greatest recruiter or motivator, but he has to be a real student of living if he is to pay the price of leadership. The price of leadership is nothing more than really living.

RAY SONNENBERG

As an avocation, Ray Sonnenberg has refereed major college basketball and football for twenty-five years and National Football League games for eleven years. He has worked with some of the most successful individuals in the world of sports—college All-Americans, Olympic Gold Medal winners, World Series heroes, and Super Bowl champions.

In this chapter, he draws an analogy of what it takes to be successful in athletics, sales, business, and life by using as examples the success stories of individuals he has known. As you read this chapter, it will motivate and inspire you to be better tomorrow than you are today. You will want to utilize your God-given talents and abilities to improve yourself and your position in life.

237

Ray Sonnenberg earned his Bachelors Degree from the School of Commerce and Finance at St. Louis University, St. Louis, Missouri as well as a Masters Degree in Administration. He is a former salesman, Sunday school teacher, YMCA Director, District Governor of Rotary International, and a member of the Illinois Basketball Hall of Fame.

He is currently vice president in charge of marketing and public relations with the MidAmerica Bank and Trust Company of Edgemont.

You may contact Ray by writing to him at 6915 West "A" Street, Belleville, IL 62223.

TO BE BETTER TOMORROW

by RAY SONNENBERG

During the past twenty-five years, it has been my privilege to be associated with some of the most successful people in the world of athletics. I've seen college All-Americans, Olympic gold medal winners, World Series heroes, and Super Bowl champions.

What makes these individuals so successful? I believe I see a common denominator in all of them, that enables them to be different, to rise above the crowd, to be successful and outstanding. Because of these qualities, they have been able to face almost certain failure and turn it into success. Even though they were beaten in the eyes of everyone but themselves, because they would not give up, because they did not know the meaning of *can't*, they persevered and emerged winners and champions.

Each of us has that hidden potential within us just like these sports heroes. I am told that the average person uses only about 10% of the talents and abilities that God has given him. One of the greatest minds the world has ever known, Albert Einstein, used only 21% of his skills and abilities. Wouldn't it be wonderful if you could find the key to turn the lock, open the door, and reach inside yourself to find an additional 5 or 10% of the talent that is stored there? If you could do this, tomorrow morning you would wake up 50% or even 100% better off than you are today. That would be fantastic, wouldn't it? To realize our full potential, we are obligated to do everything we can to be better tomorrow than we are today. Following are stories of sports greats who made themselves better each day—stories that demonstrate the four qualities of excellence: determination, dedication, desire, and persistence.

Determination

In order to realize your full potential, you must have *determination*—determination to be better tomorrow than you are today, determination to use your God-given talents and abilities to the fullest extent.

Determination can overcome a lot of things and make up for many shortcomings. One of the greatest examples of determination is the story of the young man who came into this world just like you and me, except at the end of one arm he did not have a hand like yours and mine, but rather a clump of fingers, and at the end of one leg he had only half a foot. But God, in his infinite wisdom, selected for him two special people as parents. You see, they loved their son a great deal and they forgot to tell him he was handicapped. They expected him to do everything the other kids in the neighborhood did. He had to button his shirt, tie his shoes, ride a bike, cut the grass, carry out the trash, and do other chores around the house. In grade school, he had just a taste of athletics and enjoyed it. Getting ready to start high school, he asked his mother if he could go out for football. Now what would you have said if you were his mother? "Oh no, Son, I don't want you to get hurt"? But not this young man's mother. She said, "Yes, I think it would be a good idea for you to go out for football." His father chimed in and stated that, not only did they want him to go out for the team, but they also wanted him to make the club. In order to do this, his father told him, he would have to have *determination*—more determination than anyone else out for the squad.

The young man made the freshman team, next year the sophomore team, and then the varsity team. He had such a great time playing football that, when he graduated from high school, he expressed a desire to play college football.

He looked at a number of schools and selected a small junior college in Southern California. It was a good school academically and yet not so big that he wouldn't have a chance to play on the football team.

With a great deal of hard work and determination, he made the college football team. For his efforts during the season, he was selected as an All-Conference Defensive End. Can you imagine that? A player without a hand and with only half a foot was named the best defensive end in the conference?

He had so much fun in college traveling around and playing football, that he thought he'd like to try out for a pro team. So he tried out in 1967 and was cut. Then, in 1969, the third year the New Orleans Saints were in the league, he literally walked onto the Saints' field and asked for a tryout. The second guessers, the grandstand quarterbacks, scoffed at the thought of this handicapped player making it in the NFL.

He survived every week of the preseason cuts, and when Tom Fears, the Saints' coach, selected his players to open the regular season, he was the player they called upon to open the 1969 season. He'd made it; he was now a professional football player in the National Football League, and he played in every game during that season. In fact, he was leading scorer of the Saints.

Now I want to take you up to November 8, 1970. The New Orleans Saints were playing the Detroit Lions. The Saints were ahead by the score of 16 to 14 late in the fourth quarter, which was unusual for the Saints because they didn't win many games their first two years. The Lions had the ball, marched down the field, and kicked a field goal to go ahead by the score of 17 to 16, with just 14 seconds remaining in the game.

The Lions kicked off. A Saints halfback caught the ball and advanced it up the field, only to get stopped short of the 50-yard line, with a few seconds remaining on the clock. The Saints called a time out. The coach called the young man over, put his arm around his shoulders, and said, "What do you think? Are you willing to give it a try?"

You must remember, the coach was asking him to do something that had never been done before in the history of the National Football League—to kick a field goal from this far, from the wrong side of the 50-yard line. The player pulled on his helmet, snapped his chin strap, looked the coach in the eye, and said, "Yes, Coach, I'd like to give it a try."

He ran onto the field with the placekick holder, joined the huddle, agreed upon the snap, and the team broke the huddle. The linesmen got set, the center knelt over the ball and snapped it, the placekick holder caught the ball and put it down on the turf 63 yards from the goal post. Tom Dempsey bulled his neck, sucked in his gut, took a step, and swung his leg. His foot boomed the ball in the air, and it sailed end over end for 63 yards 6 inches, just barely clearing the cross bar as Official Dick Dolack stood under the uprights and called it good. Referee Jim Tunney signalled a successful field goal, and the Saints won the game by the score of 19 to 17, as time ran out on the clock.

With that field goal, Tom Dempsey kicked himself into the NFL Record Book and possibly into the Hall of Fame. The interesting thing about it is that he didn't use his good foot. He used the bad one. Here's a guy who took his single greatest liability and turned it into his greatest asset.

I wonder how many of us have a liability not nearly as noticeable as Tom Dempsey's, that we could turn from a liability to an asset with a little bit of Tom Dempsey's determination?

Determination? I should say so! Tom Dempsey was able to find the key, turn the lock, open the door, and reach inside himself to utilize an additional 5 or 10% of his ability. He certainly followed the principle expressed in the following rhyme:

> *If you think you are beaten–you are.*
> *If you think you dare not–you don't.*
> *If you'd like to win, but you think you can't,*
> *It's almost a cinch that you won't.*
>
> *If you think you'll lose–you've lost,*
> *For out in the world you'll find*
> *Success begins with a fellow's will,*
> *It's all in the state of mind.*
>
> *If you think that you're outclassed–you are.*

You've got to think high to rise.
You've got to be sure of yourself before
You can ever win a prize.

Life's battle doesn't always go
To the swifter or faster man,
But sooner or later the man who wins
Is the man who thinks he can.

Dedication

The next quality that you have to have, the second thing that I've seen in almost every champion and winner, is *dedication*—dedicating your entire life to reaching your goals, to reaching inside yourself to become better tomorrow than you are today.

My wife and I had been in Miami—I had worked a Monday night football game, and my wife and I had planned a vacation around the job. About the middle of the week, we left for San Francisco and a game in Oakland. As we boarded the plane, my wife sat down next to a lovely silver-haired lady, and they began discussing children and athletics. The lady asked my wife if she was interested in swimming. We have a daughter that competed in the National YMCA Swimming Championships. So, for a good part of the flight across the country, the woman told us the wonderful story of her grandson.

In 1968, this young man, 18 years old, 5 feet 10 inches, and 150 pounds, went to Mexico City to compete in the Olympics. At 18, he was somewhat cocky, a little overconfident, and he'd underestimated the abilities of his opponents and the level of competition in the Olympics. He made the mistake of bragging and saying that he was going to win five gold medals—more than anyone had ever won in the Olympic games.

As the games began and he competed, it was evident that he was not going to be equal to his goal of winning five gold medals. In fact, when the last event was completed and the final scores were tallied, he was viewed as a failure by some because he had won only two gold medals. Even though that was more than some *countries* had won, he had failed to reach his goal.

In the closing ceremonies at the great stadium in Mexico City, he stood with his teammates—Old Glory was being held by a teammate just an arm's length away—and he made a decision to dedicate himself and the next four years of his life to achieving the goal that he had missed in Mexico City.

So he went home and practiced early every morning and late every night, seven days a week, all year round, except for days when he was competing in meets. He was trained so finely that he reached his peak at just the right time.

When he and his teammates went to Munich in October of 1972, he was four years older, bigger, stronger, more mature, and better poised for the competition he was about to face.

He won every race in which he competed. Not only did he win, but each time he set a new record—an American record, an Olympic record, and a world record.

When the Olympics were over, he was hailed as the greatest athlete of the Nineteenth Olympiad, for he had won seven gold medals. That's more than anyone else had ever won, and I personally can't conceive of anyone breaking that record. No one did in Montreal, and I doubt if anyone will in Moscow.

But do you know the price that Mark Spitz paid to win those seven gold medals? In preparation for those seven races, he swam over 14,000 miles. That's like jumping in the water at San Francisco, swimming to Tokyo, and then turning around and swimming back.

That's the kind of dedication it takes to be a champion, an Olympic gold medal winner, and a world record holder.

Desire

The third quality that you have to have if you're going to rise above the crowd and be successful is *desire*—desire to succeed, to be the best, to be a winner, to make the best better. The desire to accomplish something will keep you working towards your goal long after the enthusiasm fades and the commitment is forgotten.

A young man was a triple threat player for the University of Alabama football team and played on their 1937 Rose Bowl team. While he was an outstanding football player, his real desire in life was to be a major league baseball player, and he had his sights set on that goal. Suddenly the United States found itself in World War II, and he quickly found himself in uniform and in Europe, where he soon attained the rank of infantry captain. Outside a small town in Germany, he and his men were pinned down by machine-gun fire. An American tank came rumbling up the road. The captain and his crew lay in the comparative safety of a ditch by the side of the road, when the tank was struck by a shell and burst into flames. The wounded tankman tried to get out of the tank but couldn't pull himself through the hatch and fell back inside the tank.

The tank was under machine gun fire and the captain had every reason to stay in the safety of the roadside ditch, but he couldn't because a fellow soldier was in trouble inside the burning tank. He leaped out of the ditch, ran and jumped on the tracks of the tank, forced his huge frame down the hatch of the tank, and pushed the wounded soldier out of the tank. He climbed out of the tank. Just before he was ready to leap from the tank, another shell exploded, wounding him so severely that many thought he was dead.

Medics found him that evening and returned him to a hospital for treatment. After many operations and many months of hospitalization, doctors finally told him there was nothing more they could do—he'd be handicapped for life. Stunned at the news and knowing that he'd never again play baseball, he became very depressed.

With a tremendous assist from his wife, he soon readjusted to civilian life, but still missing was an important part of his life—the competitiveness of athletics. He'd been introduced to golf as part of his rehabilitation program, and when he returned home a dedicated friend encouraged him by helping with his golf game. Together they religiously practiced and played. With the assistance of this loyal friend, he again experienced the thrill and excitement of athletic competition, and his life took on new meaning.

With the desire to compete rekindled, he entered a golf tournament—a national championship golf tournament that was being played in Duluth, Minnesota, on the home course of the man who had won the same tournament the previous year. This fact didn't faze him one bit. He competed in the tournament and won the National Championship by shooting just over par. It wasn't a course record by a long shot. Probably not even the best score shot that week—but consider the fact that Charley Boswell's World War II injury had left him blind. I believe it's one of the greatest sports stories I've ever heard.

Persistence

The fourth and probably the most important of all the qualities you need to improve yourself is *persistence.* Webster defines *persistence* as the ability to go on resolutely or stubbornly in spite of difficulties, to have the tenacity not to give up or quit. Calvin Coolidge said that nothing can take the place of persistence: Talent will not! Nothing is more common than unsuccessful men with talent. Genius will not! Unrewarded genius is almost a proverb. Education will not! The world is full of educated derelicts.

Persistence is as important in life and business as it is in athletics. However, I think it is more dramatic in athletics and is called to our attention more because the ones who persist and succeed are in the limelight—they end up as our heroes. Without this valuable quality, though, they'd be just another athlete.

A young man wanted to go to college. He had his mind set on Notre Dame or Indiana, but both schools for various reasons turned him down. Somewhat discouraged, he went to another school that wasn't as well known, but it provided him an opportunity to play football and to get a college education. He performed so well that as a freshman he made the varsity and for the next four years his performance was of a high level. He set a number of records that are still in the NCAA record book today, even though he graduated over twenty years ago. He thought to himself, "I guess I showed those people that I am a good football player and that my performance was not a fluke because it was over a four-year span." But he still wasn't satisfied; he wanted to make it to the NFL and show the professionals that he was indeed one of the best players in the country. The draft came and he was again disappointed. He was selected, but only on the fifteenth round and by the team that at the time had the worst record in professional football—the Pittsburgh Steelers. The disappointment in no way dampened his enthusiasm; he worked harder than ever and reported to camp in the best condition he'd ever been in.

He played a great deal in the preseason games and survived every cut up until the final game of the preseason, but he knew a number of players for the last preseason game wouldn't be there for the opening of the regular season. He got in the game, but even though he played well, the team lost. An assistant coach called him in the next day and gave him the sad news that they were going to have to cut him, that they couldn't afford to go with a rookie. They had to go along with a veteran because they knew what the veteran could do. Discouraged and broken-hearted, the young man left the coach's office, went to his room, gathered his gear, and put it in the back of his car. He was leaving the Steelers' training camp to go home when another car approached from the opposite direction. The driver was Coach Walt Kiesling, and with him was the congenial and beloved owner of the Steelers, Art Rooney, who told the coach to stop. Rooney leaned over and through the window wished the young man well, encouraging him not to give up, to hang in there and they'd see him somewhere along the line. The two cars sped off in opposite directions, and Rooney told his coach, "You cut the wrong player. This young man has ability and the persistence you need to make a good football player."

The young man could have quit. He was a high school hero; he'd been an outstanding player in college for four years, with many NCAA records to his name. But he didn't. He went home and continued to play and practice. He called Paul Brown, then coach of the Cleveland Browns, but the Browns couldn't use him because they had a couple of excellent players in his position. This didn't discourage the young man, for he had faith in himself. He tried to catch on with other clubs, but couldn't. Then one bright sunshiny Sunday in Baltimore a player by the name of George Shaw broke his ankle, and a scout for the Baltimore Colts remembered a skinny-legged kid by the name of Johnny Unitas. For the price of a long distance phone call, the Colts picked up one of the finest gentlemen and the greatest quarterbacks ever to play in the NFL.

Our crew was working a game in Washington. As was our practice, we went to church the morning of the game. On our way, Jack Fette, who was driving, suddenly made a U-turn, drove back a block, made another U-turn, pulled up to the curb, and said to a fellow who was walking, "Come on, get in, we'll give you a ride to church." And so Johnny Unitas jumped in the car and went to church with us the morning of the game—a great player and a great gentleman.

Without persistence, Johnny Unitas would never have made it to the NFL and would never have emerged as one of the all-time great quarterbacks to play the game.

Toward Excellence in Yourself

I believe that each of you has a great deal more ability and potential than you are now using. Wouldn't it be great if you could reach inside and find that extra 5 or 10% of your ability that's stored there just waiting to be used? I hope that each of you has the *determination* of a Tom Dempsey, a sizable portion of the *dedication* of a Mark Spitz, the *desire* of a Charlie Boswell, and a generous amount of the *persistence* of a Johnny Unitas. If you do, you can't help but be successful, whether you're a salesman or surgeon, carpenter or clerk, plumber or painter.

INTRODUCING
THE EDITOR:
DONALD M. DIBLE

Don Dible presents more than 100 speeches, seminars and workshops a year all across the United States under the sponsorship of universities, trade associations, chambers of commerce, business magazines, professional societies and private companies.

His lucid, enthusiastic, experience-backed presentations are designed to inspire and motivate seminar participants and convention audiences to put to immediate use the highly-practical information he covers.

In preparing his talks, Don draws from a rich and varied background. He received his BSEE from MIT and an MSEE from Stanford University. Prior to launching his first business in 1971, he served in engineering and sales management capacities with three companies, including a subsidiary of the SCM Corporation where he was responsible for directing and training a large national sales organization producing millions of dollars in sales annually.

In the past seven years, Don has founded eight successful businesses in the publishing, advertising, seminar, graphic art services, and real estate industries. All but one of these companies was started on a part-time basis with modest capital resources. Each of Mr. Dible's businesses reflect the unusual and innovative approach he takes to sales, marketing and finance—topics discussed in detail during his many seminars and talks.

While Don is still blazing new trails in his speaking career, he is perhaps best known for his work in the field of publishing.

Prior to writing his 100,000-copy bestseller, *Up Your OWN Organization!*, Don had never written a single word for publication in his life. Aside from writing themes, book reports and term papers in high school and college, his only major writing project was a highly technical undergraduate thesis at the Massachusetts Institute of Technology.

After working for seven years in industry, Don became frustrated with the rigidly structured world of big business. He looked longingly and lovingly at the outside world of entrepreneurship—and decided to launch his own business.

Following three years of research, including attendance at numerous seminars, interviews with hundreds of successful small business owner/managers, and a thorough review of the small business books in print at the time, (mostly dry-as-a-bone textbooks and rah-rah get-rich-quick books), he finally decided that the most needed new product in the marketplace was a *realistic* book about starting a new business. Faithful to his commitment, he raised the needed capital; and with the assistance of his dedicated wife, he started The Entrepreneur Press. Next he hired a secretary, and in just four months produced a 750-page manuscript for *Up Your OWN Organization!*, with an

Introduction by Robert Townsend, former Chairman of the Board of Avis Rent-a-Car and bestselling author of *Up The Organization*. Don's second book is titled *The Pure Joy of Making More Money.*

Shortly after the publication of his first book, Don was asked to assist a professional society in organizing and presenting a two-day conference utilizing the services of fourteen attorneys, accountants, business consultants and financial executives. The program was recorded, the recordings were transcribed, and he edited and adapted the transcripts into manuscript form. The resulting book was titled *Winning The Money Game—How to Plan and Finance a Growing Business.*

As a result of the success of his company, The Entrepreneur Press, Don has published (or is in the process of publishing) the following books: *Up Your OWN Organization; Winning the Money Game; Everybody's Tooth Book; The Pure Joy of Making More Money; How to Make Money in Your Own Small Business; Fundamentals of Recordkeeping and Finance for the Small Business; What Everybody Should Know about Patents, Trademarks and Copyrights; Business Startup Basics;* and *The Official U.S. Export-Import Guide.*

Recently, Don founded a new publishing enterprise, the Showcase Publishing Company, dedicated to multi-author motivational and inspirational self-help books. This book is the inaugural volume of this company.

Finally, Don has been a guest on scores of television and radio talk shows, inluding NBC's "Monitor" with Bill Cullen, and ABC's award-winning "Mike Wallace at Large." He is also a frequent contributor to magazines such as *Dun's Review, Success Unlimited, MBA Magazine, Free Enterprise,* and *Boardroom Reports.*

You may contact Don by writing to 3422 Astoria Circle, Fairfield, California 94533, or by telephoning (707) 422-6822.

This book was designed and produced
by George Mattingly, Berkeley.
The book was typeset in Trump Mediaeval
with Friz Quadrata display
by Robert Sibley, San Francisco.
This first edition was printed and bound
by R.R. Donnelley & Sons Company
Crawfordsville, Indiana.